Honest Sadness

Lament in a Pandemic Age

— JOHN HOLDSWORTH —

Sacristy
Press

Sacristy Press
PO Box 612, Durham, DH1 9HT

www.sacristy.co.uk

First published in 2021 by Sacristy Press, Durham

Copyright © John Holdsworth 2021
The moral rights of the author have been asserted.

All rights reserved, no part of this publication may be reproduced or transmitted in any form or by any means, electronic, mechanical photocopying, documentary, film or in any other format without prior written permission of the publisher.

Scripture quotations, unless otherwise stated, are from the New Revised Standard Version Bible: Anglicized Edition, copyright © 1989, 1995 National Council of the Churches of Christ in the United States of America. Used by permission. All rights reserved worldwide.

Scripture quotations marked "REB" are from the Revised English Bible, copyright © Cambridge University Press and Oxford University Press 1989. All rights reserved.

Every reasonable effort has been made to trace the copyright holders of material reproduced in this book, but if any have been inadvertently overlooked the publisher would be glad to hear from them.

Sacristy Limited, registered in England & Wales, number 7565667

British Library Cataloguing-in-Publication Data
A catalogue record for the book is available from the British Library

ISBN 978-1-78959-161-3

Contents

Preface iv

Chapter 1. Martyr Square 1
Chapter 2. Kofinou Camp 20
Chapter 3. Curlew Close 38
Chapter 4. Bosnia 55
Chapter 5. Baghdad 73
Chapter 6. Newport Gwent 91
Chapter 7. Lancashire 109
Chapter 8. Craig y Nos Hospital 129
Postscript: The questions we all long to ask 146

Bibliography 149
Notes 154

Preface

What does the word "lament" summon up in your imagination? I see rows of gravestones in Aberfan with Karl Jenkins' "Lament for the Valley", part of his *Cantata Memoria*, playing in the background. If I listen carefully, I can hear the haunting Welsh hymn tune *Tyddyn Llwyn*, which sounds to me like sighs of anguish set to music; or perhaps a Scottish piper, playing a mournful tune on the site of an ancient bloody battlefield. I hear an Irishman singing "The Foggy Dew", a song that derives from a perceived atrocity, sung with the real feeling of someone with a stake in that. When it comes to words, my mind is drawn to poems such as the "Laments" of Gillian Clarke or Dylan Thomas. What do those associations have in common? I think we'd recognize regret, anger, pathos, deep sadness. The Old Testament book Lamentations contains all those feelings, but it is also purposeful. It describes something beyond anger: something that raises profound questions about meaning. I have called it "faithful incomprehension", and that too has contemporary traction. Historic events such as slavery or holocaust, and more recent ones such as 9/11, the AIDS phenomenon and the COVID-19 pandemic, have each resulted in "faithful incomprehension"; as do experiences of abuse, severe chronic illness, untimely bereavement and betrayal. These are challenges to our carefully constructed worldviews; and so, challenges for those of us who want to maintain religious faith and continue to see a role for the Church, both pastorally and intellectually.

    This book is an attempt to make connections between lived experience today and those biblical texts of lament. In writing it, I have drawn on my own experience from situations of modern suffering in places such as Baghdad, Beirut and Bosnia. I have also been writing within a context of personal bereavement, following the death of my wife of almost fifty years, after six years of journeying together through the unenviable world of Lewy body dementia. The question I have sought to answer was prompted by something that the Old Testament scholar Walter Brueggemann wrote: he said that the value of Lamentations in the Bible was that it served as an antidote to denial and an invitation to the faithful to be "communities of honest sadness".[1] I want to know what such a community actually looks like nowadays, and what it might mean to be part of it.

I am intrigued by the role of lament in today's world and today's Church. The ideas that cluster around this concept remind me of key issues in Christian ministry and theology. From a pastoral perspective, I want to know what response those who lament are demanding. What does lament achieve? How can we understand and meet the needs of those who lament, as friends, pastors, comforters? I recognize denial when I see it. I have experienced denial in pastoral situations, particularly of bereavement. The popularity at funerals of reading part of a sermon by Henry Scott Holland which begins, "Death is nothing at all", without the supporting commentary pointing out that it was meant as a parody, speaks for itself. In what sense is lament an antidote to that?

Lament connects with key theological themes. In so far as they are cries for deliverance, laments force us to think about what deliverance means today, and how—if at all—it differs from things we regularly speak and sing about in church, particularly salvation or redemption. What idea of God is contained in faithful lament? Is that an appropriate picture for us nowadays? Lament is a call for witnesses. Is that part of what discipleship demands of us? Lament is an affirmation of faith when experience is most at odds with faith, so is that something we can recognize in our everyday experience? What might a "community of honest sadness" look like today, and does the church have capacity for it?

Each chapter is earthed, initially, in the real world of lived experience. The second and main section deals with text and commentary, followed in each case by autobiographical reflection and testimony from my own journeying with sadness. Finally, there are suggestions for reflection. The book is designed for either group study or individual use. My hope is that, as with all practical theology, it may help us to a fresh reading of the texts as pastorally useful, and do so in a way that has consequences for both pastoral understanding and practice in churches, and for individuals.

The book falls into three natural sections. Chapters 1–4 deal with Old Testament texts. Chapters 5 and 6 are concerned with the New Testament, asking what happened to lament, which seems virtually absent there. Chapters 7 and 8 look at some contemporary situations and seek to define what the Church as a place of honest sadness might look like.

It is important to say that this is not a quest for answers to questions about why people suffer (often unjustly). Rather, it accepts suffering as a fact and sees lament as keeping us to that focus, instead of wandering into the philosophical and theological marshlands of speculation and fantasy in a quest for meaning. The 2014 film, *The Giver*, based on a bestselling book by Lois Lowry published in 1993, describes a future society in which there is no pain or suffering. But this is no utopia—in fact, it is a definite and chilling *dys*topia in which the price paid for painlessness has been the creation of a society in which there is no emotion or relationship, no memory and no choice. That is the alternative to suffering, and a commentary on the assertion that suffering is part of what makes us human. It is this realistic acceptance that makes lament stand out, and renders its absence in current religious culture so curious. Suffering is best studied, not as a philosophical concept, but through the experience of those who suffer. This book takes that experience and the biblical literature describing it and asks, what use is lament in our churches and in the lives of the faithful today?

I would like to thank Dr Rima Nasrallah, who first put the idea into my head, and the learning community of the Diocese of Cyprus and the Gulf, on whom some of the material was "tested". Professor Leslie Francis has been an invaluable critical friend, as ever. Dr Natalie Watson, Publishing Director at Sacristy Press, has kept my enthusiasm alive. In dedicating the book, I want to remember in this tangible if inadequate way those who accompanied me so faithfully and pastorally in Cyprus, where I lived and worked throughout Sue's illness. They include Bishop Michael Lewis; the congregation of St Helena's, Larnaca, especially churchwarden Rowena, and Colin and Marie who sacrificed many a service to sit with Sue and make sure she got the most from it; and also Veronika, a true Friday's child. They are my witnesses.

John Holdsworth
Llansaint
The Feast of Saints Simon and Jude 2020

CHAPTER 1

Martyr Square

Experience

I have a friend who is a lecturer at the Near East School of Theology and also minister of one of the largest Protestant churches in central Beirut. Her church is situated close to the Government buildings and what was once the "Green Line" between the Muslim west and Christian east of the city. Between the two, there was a no man's land which later, after the last war, became known as Martyr Square or Liberation Square (however you want to translate the Arabic *Tahrir* Square), and has become a place of public assembly. Prior to the explosion in Beirut in August 2020, it had become a place of public protest. I was interested to hear my friend describe, not long before the explosion, how this place had developed its purpose. Originally the protest was about corruption and the lack of reliable public services, but over the months it had become the focus for other kinds of complaint. The disabled were there on their crutches; cancer patients were demonstrating for affordable treatments; migrant workers wanted justice and equality; the elderly wanted to be noticed; gay and transgender people wanted to be accepted. This has had quite an effect on the context of churchgoing. She went on to say this:

> As we stubbornly gathered in my church Sunday after Sunday defying roadblocks and burning tyres, the soundtrack of our worship was of unspeakable curses, screaming and banging of pots and pans outside our windows. Screams and curses often turned into sobs and tears. People had found in that square a place, not only to speak up against injustice, but also to lament. To lament the unfairness of life. To lament their wounded lives. Broken marriages. Failing health. Loneliness.

What strikes me about that description is, first of all, the use of the word "lament" to describe this phenomenon of anguished complaint; and second, the juxtaposition of the lamenting community and the worshipping one. Knowing my friend, I am sure that she has not missed the opportunity this juxtaposition provides to reflect on what it means to be a church in this setting, but we do not all have that opportunity presented in such an immediate way.

One example of an unexpected—and in its way traumatic—event, closer to home for many of us, has been the COVID-19 pandemic. This event has had huge repercussions on how we order our lives. Early in 2020, pundits were already telling us that there would in future be a BC and an AC: "before COVID" and "after COVID". This was going to be a watershed event that would bring about a reassessment of working practices, patterns of living and travelling, and indeed of our need for social life and how that could be preserved. And those changes have proved difficult enough to cope with. But there has also been more immediate cause for lament: people have died prematurely and unexpectedly. There has been a sense that some of these deaths were avoidable and someone must answer for them. People who had been working valiantly to help others through the crisis (in the health services, for example) became victims. During the first wave, there was the shocking and cruel irony that *care* homes were the very places where people were dying. Funerals could not be held, nor grief publicly shared and expressed. Mental health problems proliferated. A new sense of "my neighbour is my enemy" fed a growing culture of social suspicion.

What our own experience does not provide, the creative arts of drama, literature and poetry may draw us into. Each genre has its own formal rules which can be employed to great effect. The First World War, when thousands of conscript soldiers were dying in awful squalor less than a hundred miles from Britain's shores, whilst life went on largely undisturbed in Britain itself, provided a juxtaposition that has offered material for poets and novelists ever since. The title of Sebastian Faulks' 1993 novel *Birdsong* is itself reminiscent of lament: in this case, the lament of all creation. But the most prolific writers were the ones we now call the "war poets". Their poems are brutal in their descriptions and demand a reassessment, a reshaping of meaning in the world. A famous example is

Wilfred Owen's "Dulce et Decorum Est", referring to a line from a Latin Ode: "It is a sweet and fitting thing to die for your country"—a sentiment found in popular Great War recruiting literature:

> Bent double, like old beggars under sacks,
> Knock-kneed, coughing like hags, we cursed through sludge,
> Till on the haunting flares we turned our backs
> And towards our distant rest began to trudge.
> Men marched asleep. Many had lost their boots
> But limped on, blood-shod. All went lame; all blind;
> Drunk with fatigue; deaf even to the hoots
> Of tired, outstripped Five-Nines that dropped behind.
>
> Gas! Gas! Quick, boys!—An ecstasy of fumbling,
> Fitting the clumsy helmets just in time;
> But someone still was yelling out and stumbling
> And flound'ring like a man in fire or lime . . .
> Dim, through the misty panes and thick green light,
> As under a green sea, I saw him drowning.
>
> In all my dreams, before my helpless sight,
> He plunges at me, guttering, choking, drowning.
>
> If in some smothering dreams you too could pace
> Behind the wagon that we flung him in,
> And watch the white eyes writhing in his face,
> His hanging face, like a devil's sick of sin;
> If you could hear, at every jolt, the blood
> Come gargling from the froth-corrupted lungs,
> Obscene as cancer, bitter as the cud
> Of vile, incurable sores on innocent tongues,—
> My friend, you would not tell with such high zest
> To children ardent for some desperate glory,
> The old Lie: *Dulce et decorum est*
> *Pro patria mori.*

What is striking in these war poems is their description of reality, contrasted with theoretical concepts of glory and valour. We see in Owen's poem the ugly language and the barely suppressed anger of the one following that cart, into which the body was simply flung.

Text and commentary

Lamentations

We can recognize that same trait in the poems contained in the Old Testament book of Lamentations. Although Lamentations is the English name for this book, it has a different name in Hebrew. In English Bibles, it is sometimes called the Lamentations of Jeremiah, and it comes immediately after the Book of Jeremiah. In the Hebrew Bible it is found between Ruth and Ecclesiastes; when the Old Testament was translated into Greek, it was repositioned, with a new initial verse: "And it came to pass, after Israel was taken captive, and Jerusalem made desolate, that Jeremias sat weeping, and lamented and said . . . " The opening word of the book in Hebrew sounds more like a primordial scream— "*Eikhaaah!*" It simply means "How?" as in "How on earth?" And "How", in Hebrew, for Jews, is the name of the book. How on earth! How, indeed. Lamentations consists of a series of five short poems describing a ruined city, laid waste as a result of what we would now call war. These poems have that in common with those written during and after the First World War.

Lamentations is not a treatise about suffering. It asks the question, "How?" and not the question, "Why?" Of course, it has a link with suffering, but in an intensely practical way. The theologian Dorothee Solle puts it like this: "The first step towards overcoming suffering is, then, to find a language that leads out of the uncomprehended suffering that makes one mute, a language of lament, of crying, of pain, a language that at least says what the situation is."[2] Lament is pragmatic. Although the form of lament in Lamentations is poetry, a modern reader might like to think of what is described in terms of a TV documentary. The five chapters introduce us to a series of pictures and voices. The pictures are quite familiar to us. We see images of devastated cities quite regularly on our screens, and even the voices are easy to imagine as they describe inhuman horrors. The narrator (the first voice we hear) is like a documentary presenter, showing us scenes of destruction, not to assemble an argument, but something more powerful: to arouse us to consider the tragic story of it all, and to realize the complexity of situations like this. We are presented, in other words, with data to process. Modern TV documentaries often assume the role of challenging an audience that wants to see everything in terms of black and white and to have simple solutions. At their best, TV documentaries that simply present to us the voices and the pictures break into those easy solutions, and prompt us to do more work. In a postmodern way, they urge us to consider that truth may not be plain and simple, but complicated and varied. In the situation addressed by Lamentations, the main complication is the role of God.

What does the text say?
In Chapter 1, we begin with a chillingly unemotional narrator describing a city's plight, to which the reader is invited to be a witness. The city is Jerusalem, and it lies in ruins. The story begins at night, like much literature that anticipates a bad outcome. It is full of atmosphere. It tells the story of Jerusalem as the story of a woman, and indeed women feature regularly in the poems. "She weeps bitterly in the night, with tears on her cheeks; ... she has no one to comfort her" (1:2). It is easier, somehow, to describe the enormity of victimhood by recounting the experience of women and using female images. Jerusalem has been raped. At 1:5, we see an early example of the "on the one hand, on the other" method of presentation, "The LORD has made her suffer for the multitude of her transgressions." Yes, we may say, sin deserves its reward. Then immediately afterwards, "her children have gone away, captives before the foe". And we are made to think again. Is this proportionate? Does any sin, especially a sin that a whole people is said to have committed, justify children being taken away from their mother?

The voice changes to that of the woman herself. Following a long catalogue of the dreadful things God has done, we hear her say (1:18), "The LORD is in the right, for I have rebelled against his word;" and we are uneasy, because this sounds suspiciously like the voice of abused women the world over: it was my fault—I deserved it. Is God an abuser? From the beginning we are challenged to think about the nature of God. One of the features of this book is that God does not speak; we never hear God's voice. We put together a picture of God from the cries of the afflicted, and it is not an attractive picture. "The speakers rarely attempt to appease God, and they do not spare God. Although they offer contradictory testimonies, the predominant opinion among them is that God is cruel and violently abusive."[3] If we can offer no further commentary we might as well close the Bible at this point. "If God is abusive, victims of abuse are without refuge, tyrants and bullies cannot be restrained, and love can never be trusted." A great deal is at stake here.

When we read further, in Chapter 2 the narrator becomes more involved. He accuses and blames God. On behalf of the women, he implores God to look what God has done:

> Look, O LORD, and consider!
> To whom have you done this?
> Should women eat their offspring,
>   the children they have borne?
> Should priest and prophet be killed
>   in the sanctuary of the Lord?
>
> *Lamentations 2:20*

And then, in chapter 3, we see something different. There is a different memory of God. Hope appears:

> The steadfast love of the LORD never ceases,
>   his mercies never come to an end;
> they are new every morning;
>   great is your faithfulness.
>
> The LORD is good to those who wait for him,
>   to the soul that seeks him.
> It is good that one should wait quietly
>   for the salvation of the LORD.
>
> *Lamentations 3:22,23,25,26*

The striking fact is that hope comes at this point, in the middle of the book, and not as a happy ending. Because hope fades as soon as it arises. It is just one more voice among the many. Its disappearance is part of the cruelty. But that, surely, is also part of human experience. The writer Evelyn Underhill once said that life would be perfectly bearable were it not for those few brief moments of happiness. In the midst of suffering hope can often appear, only to be dashed, making the cruelty even worse. But the appearance of hope also gives voice to the faith of those suffering. It's as if they are saying that although their experience does not match their faith, nevertheless their experience cannot be denied, and they are determined to state their faith in a kind of "This I know" sort of way. This I know: the Lord is good. This I know: the Lord's compassion is new every morning. This I know: rejection by the Lord does not last for ever. And the pathetic but realistic, "The Lord is all that I have" (3:24 REB). These take on the form of a mantra, and such mantras are important. When all the landmarks are vanishing, there needs to be some way of articulating faith. Its voice needs to be heard.

There is something quite modern about how Chapter 4 is presented. We imagine our film crew touring the streets of the city, picking out the face of a child here and a woman there. The narrator tells the almost unimaginable horror of what these people have been reduced to:

> With their own hands tender-hearted women
>   boiled their own children;
> their children became their food
>   on the day of my people's wounding.
>
> *Lamentations 4:10 (REB)*

And then in verses 17–22, the people clamour towards the camera, each shouting, just wanting to be heard:

> When we go out, we take to by-ways
>   to avoid the public streets;
> our days are all but finished,
>   our end has come.
>
> *Lamentations 4:18 (REB)*

What better example of chaos can there be than that of women who have completely lost any maternal instinct? Every social structure seems to be broken. The speakers appear hopeless, exhausted and resigned. Chapter 5 just fades away; there is nothing left, no passion, no resistance, only bleak despair and resignation. The final plea is a prayer. Faith persists pathetically:

> Restore us to yourself, O LORD, that we may be restored;
>   renew our days as of old—
> unless you have utterly rejected us,
>   and are angry with us beyond measure. (5:21,22).

So what does this biblical book, Lamentations, tell us about lament?

- This book's triumph is that it tells a recognizable and realistic story of human experience of suffering. It conveys the sense of confusion, of immediacy, of incomprehension, vulnerability and fear.
- The voices that are crying out for a pastoral response have a contemporary ring, saying things like, "God is cruel. I am bereft. My life is shattered, and my hopes are wrecked. How could God do this to me? What have I done to deserve this?" But the response of the sufferers is ambiguous because we also hear that God was right. "We have done wrong. We deserve all this."
- There is no attempt at resolution or move towards closure. Lament represents a provisional stage.
- In giving the sufferer a voice, the book provides a witness. This is the first thing the sufferers want. They want an opportunity to speak for themselves and to tell it like it feels and seems, and to be heard, and they want confirmation of their grief.
- What it does not do, at least on the face of it, is to give God an opportunity to speak. God's voice is the one voice that is missing. All we hear about God are the people's assumptions about God. And for the modern reader, it is those assumptions that make us uneasy. What exactly lies behind the voice we hear at 3:33, "for he does not willingly afflict or grieve anyone."?

We need to put this book into various contexts. What had happened to create this scene of devastation? The historic context reads like this: Jerusalem, God's HQ, had come under successive attack from Babylonian forces in 597 and 587 BCE, and then in a final round-up in 586, following an attempted coup. It was, as they say, laid waste. Most of its inhabitants were taken to exile in Babylon (modern Iraq). So began the experience which is called simply "The Exile", and which lasted for three generations. The theological context is one in which the reflective community of faith is trying to make sense of their experience of the Exile, after the event. How could a God who promised land, progeny and a special relationship with a chosen people allow them to be taken from the land, to risk losing their special identity in a foreign land, and to suffer? Jerusalem was God's special place—it was the most important city in all that was left of the greater land of Israel. Split into two separate states after the time of King Solomon, the northern one had been overcome by Assyria in the eighth century BCE and only the tiny southern "state" of Judah was left. Now this too was gone. Was there a theological message in all this? Competing views emerged as the community of faith sought to make theological sense of it all. But at its heart were the raw facts and emotions, and that is what lament presents us with.

Shattered narratives
Perhaps the translators were right to place Lamentations next to Jeremiah, because it does belong initially to his time and context, though not written by him. But like all biblical writings, its meaning and application are not exhausted by its initial context. The point is that those Old Testament writings about the Exile have contemporary significance in any situation where fundamental beliefs about God, purpose, meaning and destiny are called into question, and where some or other event causes us to have to draw a line under the reassuring past and move towards an uncertain future. The book of Lamentations, as one of the "scrolls" ("*megilloth*"), is read annually at the Jewish remembrance (usually in June or July) of all the terrible things that have happened throughout the history of the Jewish people. In our turn, we might also speak of 9/11, of the AIDS epidemic in Africa, of massacres in Rwanda or Srebrenica, of slavery, of pandemics like COVID-19 or that other pandemic which, 100 years ago,

killed fifty million people across the world. We could add other events from history to that list. They are all events that can affect our individual faith. In our personal lives also, things happen that cause the same kind of trauma for us: that cause us to question everything we thought we had known and trusted about God. These are events that leave us initially baffled, speechless, vulnerable, afraid and insecure, not knowing how the future will unfold and what our place in it will be. They are events prompting the view that things will never be the same again.

We must not lose sight of the fact that Lamentations is in the canon of Scripture because it is the legacy of those who wanted to maintain faith. This book is not a dismissal of faith. The speakers here do not share the cynical and disillusioned view of the war poets who believed faith itself to be a lie. Laments are expressions of what I want to call "faithful incomprehension". They are addresses to God (some might call them prayers, but that only works if we redefine what we mean by prayer, to accommodate their form and content); but the very fact that their subjects feel able to complain to God is, in itself, an act of fidelity. It is strange for us to hear faith expressed in such ugly language. Brueggemann counters any supposed embarrassment about that language. He describes how lament turns to rage in one of the lament psalms, Psalm 137:

> With such texts, the church need not engage in pious cover-up or false assurance. This psalm in its rage is an act of "catching up" with new reality. If Zion's songs are to be sung, it will be a long, long way from all old "Zions." The psalmist is beginning to engage that tough but undeniable reality.[4]

We want church to be nice, available to the most naive and childlike, so how do we combine that with a very adult and grimly realistic view of life? It is as if, back at the situation in Beirut, we might wish they would shut up outside and let us get on with singing songs about gratefulness and plenty. Lamentations gives us no such escape.

Lamentations as an antidote to denial
Kathleen O'Connor, a colleague of Brueggemann's, has made a special study of Lamentations and sees the book as having a wider reference

than the streets of sixth-century BCE Jerusalem, or modern Aleppo. She believes society (American and Western) is characterized by denial—a denial evidenced by consumerism, escapism, addiction and violence:

> Lamentations refuses denial, practices truth-telling, and reverses amnesia. It invites readers into pain, chaos, and brutality, both human and divine. It conveys effects of trauma, loss, and grief beyond tears. Because God's voice is absent, it gives primacy to suffering voices like no other biblical book.[5]

For her, denial is a failing—a sin, even—endemic in humankind, and so Lamentations counts as good news in its denial of denial. O'Connor's theological reflection is deeply personal and pastoral. She says, "Lamentations has helped me to claim my inner world and calls me outward to the sufferings of the world."[6] The picture she paints of the book is of a community of people with common grief each having a turn to articulate it, perhaps (though she does not make the connection) rather like an Alcoholics Anonymous meeting. She sees this as an example of how truth is voiced in a postmodern world, and perhaps that points to one aspect of what a community of honest sadness might look like.

A key theological term for her is *witness*. Lamentations shows reverence for the voice of the afflicted. She notes how the narrator moves, between Chapters 1 and 2, from being dispassionate to becoming the "impassioned advocate" for the Daughter of Zion: "Because the narrator sees the enormity of her pain, he is her comforter and her witness."[7] O'Connor notes how difficult it is for us to hear this pain expressed. We want to intervene with some sight of green shoots. She quotes one father who lost his nineteen-year-old son in a climbing accident: "If you think your task as comforter is to tell me that really, all things considered, it's not so bad, you do not sit with me in my grief but place yourself off in the distance away from me."[8] In Lamentations 1:12 the Daughter of Zion asks, "Look and see if there is any sorrow like my sorrow?" Finding the answer "Yes" would not be helpful. Instead, at 2:13 we hear the response of the narrator: "To what can I compare you for your comfort, virgin daughter of Zion? For your wound gapes as wide as the ocean . . . " (REB). Only the infinite can be compared with the infinite without one diminishing the other. And the poetic form is the one that best enables and gives the capacity to mirror pain across the ages. This is uncomfortable reading for those would-be pastors who feel that they must bring good news and hope—clumsily—to every situation.

O'Connor believes that suffering people have a gift to pass on to us, which she describes as the gift of their own humanity. "[T]hey show us our own need of healing."[9] She speaks from a North American culture, of which she is critical in regard to its capacity to deny pain. "Denial interferes with our ability to accept the pain of others,"[10] and so it gets in the way of compassion and of the positive value of Lamentations, which is to suggest a role for liturgy and to make a space for justice to be born.[11]

> Lamentations should have a central place in worship, because it can be a mirroring witness for those who live with untold sorrow and doubt. It can be a treasure stored in our spirits for the days to come. It can lead us through our sorrow and connect us in compassion to our neighbours. It provides a web of words, images and vignettes that can in turn spawn new laments.[12]

What O'Connor points to, as the appropriate pastoral response, is to be one who listens and absorbs and gives respect to the suffering; one who is prepared to let compassion prompt action for justice. "Prayers of lament in general and Lamentations in particular make space for justice to be born."[13]

Lament and salvation

A different approach to the Old Testament texts of lament and their contemporary significance is that of the German scholar Claus Westermann.[14] He begins by attempting to place lament within the theological understanding of the people of Israel. He believes it belongs in the recurring story of deliverance, or as we might want to term it, salvation. He notes that whenever the history of Israel's deliverance from Egypt is told, it follows a certain pattern. Deuteronomy 26:5–11 is typical, following this pattern: prehistory (26:5); distress (26:6); call for help (26:7a); which God hears (26:7b); the leading out from slavery and oppression, and leading into the promised land (26:8,9); and the (obligatory) response of rejoicing (26:10,11). The cry for help—the lament—therefore has a central place in the sequence of salvation. The importance of this is obscured to modern western theology, in Westermann's view, because we want theology to be about absolutes such as "God" and "humankind", whereas the Old Testament sees the important theological content in the speech event between them. Laments are "an essential part of what the Old Testament says happened between God and man".[15]

Westermann is keen to point out just how natural lament was within this conversation, and how unnatural it now seems to us. Lament deals with basic data in a matter-of-fact way. Exodus 3:7,8 (for example) simply states that the people are suffering—without explanation—and that God responds, again without justification. Lament simply implores God to be compassionate to those who suffer. Suffering often involves a sense of broken relationship, and for Old Testament people, speaking of a break in their relationship with God is tantamount to expressing the loss of a sense of meaning, and that must be acknowledged. Sin may be the acknowledged reason for the break in relationship, and some (though few) laments are media for expressing guilt (e.g. Psalms 51, 130). Old Testament people take for granted a view of God as being in control of their destinies. Suffering must have a cause. Sin is the obvious candidate, and the confession of sin is a rational response. But most laments speak from faithful incomprehension. The suffering experienced appears not to be part of a rational system. Westermann notes that when guilt is confessed in the Psalms, it always refers to specific actions and occasions. In the New Testament, and especially in the Letters of Paul, sin is described rather, as part of the human condition: "a lamenter appears before God as one who is guilty."[16]

Any attempt to find a modern equivalent for content in lament that begins with the Old Testament theology of salvation is going to end with the frustration that Westermann professes. In the Old Testament, Israel's initial understanding of salvation and deliverance is part of a story about *actually* being delivered from one place of oppression and settled in another of peace and plenty. That is a story particular to Israel's recounted and remembered history, but even as the Old Testament progresses, despite the liturgical attempts to keep the story and memory alive, it becomes more difficult—for a nation now settled and relatively prosperous and developed—to see salvation as something necessary in the present. Whereas it is easy to see what an enslaved and oppressed people need to be delivered from, and what a promised land of their own would mean to them, it is much more difficult for a settled and relatively successful people to answer the questions, "What do you need to be delivered from?" and "What do you yearn to be settled to?" There are many modern examples of this phenomenon which will spring to mind. In British history, people from Tolpuddle in Dorset were martyred because of their stand on workers' rights; a whole movement looks back to that occasion as it charts its history towards the legally enshrined employment rights of nowadays. But attempts to rekindle that spirit of revolutionary zeal for justice can seem rather confected in modern trades union rhetoric, notwithstanding that there is still plenty of injustice to fight. The shipyard workers of Gdansk in Poland yearned to be free of Communist control, and flocked to church as a place where they felt their grievances were understood and could be articulated safely. But once their democracy was established, church attendance fell away. There was no need to be revolutionaries any longer.

In the Old Testament context there had to be a move in thinking about salvation, from the particular to the universal. One answer was to see *sin* as that from which we need to be delivered. Sin is certainly a universal condition. By the time of the New Testament, texts which once referred to actual liberation from actual oppression now become adapted to being delivered from our body of sin (Romans 7:23–25). Another answer is to see *oppression* as the universal condition from which people need to be freed, and so to see salvation referring to those peoples who are oppressed in our world today, who can identify in a different way with the texts. That leads to a different application of the story—in what has come to be known as "liberation theology"—to any number of situations. Some are very similar to the Old Testament context in which one nation or tribe or people is oppressed by another. Others are quite different, dealing with a wider range of justice and inclusion issues. These are often viewed with suspicion by some branches of the Christian family, who want to make a distinction between religion and politics that the Old Testament does not allow. Being "the Israel of God" (Galatians 6:16) can become a purely spiritual concept, and the answer to the question, "Saved for what?" comes to be answered again in spiritual terms that rarely refer to this life. It is no wonder, in that context, that lament has such a limited place.

So lament, as well as having a pastoral function, also plays its part in whatever we mean by salvation. It is the way in which God hears the people's plight, and so is crucial in effecting change.

Poems and pain
Is the *form* of lament important? F. W. ("Chip") Dobbs-Allsopp approaches the text of Lamentations from a literary critical perspective.[17] Seamus Heaney quoted Hugh MacDiarmid's description of poetry as "human existence come to life", and that is exactly what these poems do. They bring human existence, human experience to life and to notice. They have a very formal structure and are arranged in multiples of twenty-two lines—the number of letters in the Hebrew alphabet. In the first four poems there are acrostics: that is, each line begins with the successive letters of the Hebrew alphabet. This is obvious to the reader, in English translation, only in the *New Jerusalem Bible*. Some of the poems follow the conventions of a funeral dirge, beginning with this very striking word in Hebrew, "How?" That is the ever-present question or resigned exclamation of the poems. Some older scholars thought the poems were simply a gathered anthology. More recently, scholars have seen them as a carefully arranged and structured unity. But the point is, is the very formal and dirge-like structure of lament particularly appropriate to its message?

Dobbs-Allsopp believes so. He notes that this is a form conducive to postmodern ideas of truth, in that it consists of a series of poetic statements without systematic coherence. We are not to look for a systematic theology here, but rather for a series of fragments, perhaps even contradictory or juxtaposed fragments, which combine to create an impression. Literary critics are concerned with the effect of the text on the reader. The choice of poetry is a form particularly well suited to eliciting an emotional response from the reader. "These poems [in the book of Lamentations] construct compassion in their readers,"[18] and by refusing to grant any one point of view precedence, engender reflection.

Humans need to grieve, and Lamentations gives grieving people both permission to do so and a vocabulary to use. The question posed at 1:12 is: "Are we passers-by, or are we witnesses?"

Personal response

Few readers of Lamentations will feel like passers-by, and I certainly don't. In its call for witnesses I see my own need to share what has been private, as I have had to fight denial and to accept that certain things are over, never to be repeated, including things that gave my life purpose and meaning. Perhaps a word of autobiographical context might be useful.

Sue and I met at university. She did a degree in History, and I was supposedly doing one in English and Philosophy, though I spent most of my time editing the university newspaper in preparation (as I expected it) for a career in journalism. She was a committed Anglican, and I a lapsed Methodist, but it became clear that if the relationship was going to go anywhere, I needed to have a Damascus Road conversion (with hopes that I could perhaps have it reversed later). But it didn't work out like that, and I suppose in those days I saw the hand of God in what you might call both the horizontal and the vertical relationships. I got ordained, and we married. For each of us, this was the only serious relationship we had known. Our adolescence lasted well into our sixties. Our relationship was intensely loving and fulfilling in every way, and we never lost that sense of youthful delight in one another. We had plans for retirement. And then our narrative was shattered, and I am still coming to terms with a future that represents such a traumatic break with the past. We had been a couple for fifty years.

Sue did not "go gentle into her good night". For me, it was not so much an event as a process that slowly ground away at my narrative. It was the process, over some six years, of watching my wife succumb to a particularly virulent form of dementia. We are used to stories of dementia patients who have vascular dementia or Alzheimer's syndrome. The ones we see are old, doddery and frail—they seem to fade away into incomprehension quite serenely. That is not how Lewy body dementia works. It includes aspects of just about every mental illness you can mention, including psychosis, depression, anxiety, bipolar disorder, Parkinson's disease. It is accompanied by lack of empathy, aggression and outright violence. My wife was athletic, active and vivacious. She had incredible patience for—and sympathy with—mentally ill people with whom she worked for a good part of her life. Although in her mid-sixties, she could easily have been taken for someone ten years younger. One friend described us as "a golden couple" who had everything going for them and perfectly complemented each other. In Larnaca, Cyprus, we lived in the midst of a predominantly Greek-speaking area containing everything that the term "Mediterranean" summons up. The world seemed like our oyster.

In my case, denial was made easier by the doctors' inability to identify the condition (which is notoriously difficult to diagnose). We were told first that Sue had had a psychotic incident from which she would recover completely, then that she had vascular dementia, only to be told six months later that she did not have any form of dementia. Then the suspect was a form of Parkinson's disease, with the possibility of frontal lobe dementia. Three years after the first symptoms appeared, we had the final diagnosis. Throughout that entire process, denial had given the illusion of respite, but finally denial was no longer possible. Lamenters use raw language because it is the only language appropriate for the reality of the situations they face and for truly expressing what they feel. Suffering often has ugly consequences. As the bits of the brain that govern restraint ceased to function, our whole life seemed to become more aggressive and uglier. From my own experience, I can say that to restrain someone who wants to run naked into the street outside at 2 a.m., to confront (with the most violent of language) the person only she can hear, and who she thinks is spreading slander about her, is an ugly business. Trying to silence the person who is screaming that you are killing her, in the middle of the night, so all the street can hear, is an ugly task, raising ugly feelings. To describe the sheer squalor of the process of dehumanization, only ugly words will do. To say, "It isn't fair" doesn't come close. Gentle language simply won't do. That does raise the question, though, of whose lament I am concerned with. Is it mine, which I am able to articulate but which I speak mostly on Sue's behalf, or is it the much worse lament of Sue herself that I can only guess at, unable, as she was, to vocalize it except through acts of rage? Or is it a lament at the sheer state of things that allows such human suffering without dessert or recourse or reason?

And yet, there were times I want to retain in my memory, times that were positive. I believe that we never ceased to love each other or to recognize that love in each other. And it's important to maintain that perspective. I agree with mantras. When faith no longer chimes with experience, as in Lamentations, repeating the axioms of faith in a "This I know" kind of way is not a form of denial but rather an assertion of who I really am, when that identity is in danger of getting lost. In my case, there were two mantras (if we can call them that) which I repeated many times. One derived from David Jenkins, sometime Bishop of Durham. A controversial figure, who tended to speak in academic language, he was challenged once to describe his faith in a single sentence using words of one syllable. In fact, he took two sentences and had to use one word of two syllables—Jesus—but we can forgive him that. The sentences were: "God is; He is as He is in Jesus; so there is hope. God is; He is for me; so it is worth it." The other mantra came from an old friend, Tony Crockett, who was diagnosed with cancer (which proved to be fatal) soon after his appointment as Bishop of Bangor. From his hospital bed in the Royal Marsden, he wrote a series of pastoral letters designed to be read in parishes back home in the Diocese, and to assure parishioners of his continuing prayer and concern for them. I recall one which ended in a very Mother Julian-esque kind of way: "God is good, and in the end all will be well." Those two mantras supported me in dark times, and I recognize that experience when I read Lamentations 3.

The need for a witness is more complex than it sounds. For the early years of the illness I was more concerned to safeguard Sue's privacy than to seek support by telling our story. I repressed the story to allow her some dignity. When I think back over that story now it is almost unbelievable: the violence that had trashed hundreds of euros' worth of belongings, the carefully prepared meals flung (literally) in my face, the attempts on my life, the shouting, the sobbing. But by this time the need for a witness for comfort and support had receded. It is other people who want to tell the story because what they have seen has affected them.

Yet perhaps most important are the "This I know" personal mantras about our relationship itself; the things that could not be forgotten and needed to be preserved, for survival in the future as well as now. Like the treasured photograph rescued from the ruins of a bombed-out house, it is the more treasured as a reminder because it is partly burned. Rescue and salvation are not just technical theological terms. We need to feel them, and lament—perhaps—opens the way today as it has always done.

Suggestions for reflection

- Try to imagine yourself as a part of that crowd in Beirut. What would you have been shouting about? Now imagine yourself as a member of the congregation there. How does it feel to be part of a congregation "with all that noise"? What kinds of question does that raise for you?
- How have you responded to the COVID-19 pandemic? Was the experience intensely personal, or did you feel that the whole community joined together in a common response?
- Try to get hold of some more war poetry. Read it out loud, and then read a chapter of Lamentations immediately afterwards. What similarities and differences do you see?
- Read Lamentations 4 as if you were a film director. What images would you want to shoot, to illustrate the text?
- Can you think of times in your experience when God has been silent? How did that feel?
- Have you ever wished that someone would just listen to you?

CHAPTER 2

Kofinou Camp

Experience

Amar and his family
Refugees in Cyprus mostly arrive there by accident. Some arrive in boats headed for elsewhere that are blown off course; some are landed there by unscrupulous people-traffickers who tell them, when they land, that they are in Sweden. Once in Cyprus it is almost impossible to move on, and the opportunities for settling are limited. Yet many do end up there, and one of the camps at Kofinou was where I met Amar and his family. They had started coming to my church at St Helena's in Larnaca. Though Muslim, they took the view (common amongst many Muslims, though you wouldn't get that impression from the media) that we are all "people of the book" and that you couldn't make the best the enemy of the good. I learned their backstory as I visited the camp and enjoyed their hospitality: he had worked in a shop selling phones in Damascus while she stayed at home looking after their twin boys. Bombs fell, but not on them. Life went on. Then one day some artillery hit the house next door. A wall collapsed on top of their boys, killing them both. They moved out of Damascus and fled to Turkey, where they found the local people hostile and so moved to Cyprus, where they are now marooned with little hope of resettlement—and what hope there was, set back probably years as a result of the virus pandemic. They now have another child, for which they are thankful. Amar writes to me every week and tells me that, though they are the most miserable and wretched of families, they nevertheless echo the response of the victims in Lamentations 3:24, that "the Lord is all I have" (REB). Their lives, says Amar, are in God's hands.

This kind of response raises two issues for me. The first is my sheer incredulity about how faith can persist against these odds. The second is to wonder whether the God that they have faith in bears any relation to mine. They appear still to believe in the kind of God who works according to the sequence as set out in Exodus 2:23–25 and Exodus 3:7–10. God's people suffer; God's people cry to God (lament); God notices and hears them; God decides to deliver them. God acts. This system is extended to the belief that God acts justly and always hears and acts for those who have a just cause.

The Old Testament itself questions those very things in a book called, simply, "Job". Nowadays we would call it a work of fiction in its form—a novel, perhaps, though it's not exactly holiday reading. We do not know the author, but the story he (she?) tells reminds us, first, of how it feels when you suffer a whole sequence of misfortunes, as a person who is determined to maintain faith as your main defence against complete meaninglessness. And the author continues to the much larger theme of what happens when you introduce human nature into the sequence. In other words, when you defend God along the lines of, "Actually, I deserve what happened to me because I sinned, and God is the divine guarantor of that kind of justice", that explanation simply does not accord with the human experience that sees good people suffer and bad people prosper. Even when such an advocate might claim that all good people do bad things from time to time, the suffering that might be said to result looks completely disproportionate. In other words, this is a book which starts with a lament, consequent on traumatic suffering, but which questions the whole basis on which the traditional view of lament rests.

A soldier's tale
This is a modern pastoral concern and one prompted not just by Amar and his family. You might wonder how a theology that sees God as rewarding good people and punishing bad ones could ever take hold, since it so obviously flies in the face of lived experience. One rather sinister reason could be that we authenticate it through a sense of our own guilt. This was brought home to me on one occasion when I was at camp as a chaplain with the Territorial Army. The first time I ever went away on summer camp with my regiment was immediately after I joined, so it was my

introduction to new people. We travelled to northern Europe, on what was for me the first trip I had made on an aeroplane. I was grateful, on the journey, for the company and reassurance of a well-travelled junior officer with whom I also shared the onward journey by bus. He was my first real personal contact. Eventually we arrived at our destination camp and had a chance to relax in the mess where some, including my new friend, were playing snooker. During the game I was approached by the adjutant who spoke quietly in my ear. "I'm afraid I've got a bit of a googly for you," he said (in the manner of adjutants). He mentioned the name of the man who had been my companion. "We've just had a signal that his baby son has died in an unexplained cot accident. Can you tell him, while I make arrangements to get him shipped back?"

We went for a walk outside and I broke the news. It seemed to him that this was not unexplained at all. This was God's retribution for the fact that he had been having an extramarital affair. An interesting question for reflection might be, "What should I have said next?" I suspect answers might range from "You're probably right; get down on your knees this instant." to "Your sins are forgiven. Go and sin no more." But all he really wanted to do was to lament. He wanted someone to know, and to know how he felt. And to know how he felt about God at that moment. And so, in that darkness, we tried to put a prayer together. I recall it began, "God, you're a real bastard!" Laments use ugly words.

Miserable sinners

We must realize, as well, that presenting the religious life as a relationship between a sinful humanity that deserves all it gets and a policeman-like judging God who is constantly disappointed and disapproving has many modern supporters—even modern hymns sometimes speak about the wrath of God. But this description of the religious relationship gained much new life at the time of the Reformation. Consider this prayer from Calvin's *Forms of Prayer for the Church*:

> And surely, O Lord, from the very chastisements which thou hast inflicted upon us, we know that for the justest causes thy wrath is kindled against us; for, seeing thou art a just Judge, thou afflictest not thy people when not offending. Therefore, beaten

with thy stripes, we acknowledge that we have provoked thy anger against us: and even now we see thy hand stretched forth for our punishment. The swords which thou art wont to use in inflicting vengeance are now drawn, and those with which thou threatenest sinners and wicked men we see ready to smite.

But though thou mightest take much severer punishment upon us than before, and thus inflict blows an hundredfold more numerous, and though disasters only less dreadful than those with which thou didst formerly chastise the sins of thy people of Israel, should overtake us, we confess that we are worthy of them, and have merited them by our crimes.[19]

So does lament demand such a view of our relationship with God? Challenge to that is to be found in the Old Testament itself.

Text and commentary

Before moving from the Book of Lamentations to other parts of the Old Testament, let us summarize what that book tells us about lament:

- For the suffering, lament is a cry seeking a witness, a reporter.
- Lament is the voice of the vulnerable, disorientated and frightened, but nevertheless a voice that wants to maintain faith.
- The report of lament is an antidote to apathy. Lament demands compassionate response.
- Communal lament is evidence of a community that is not in denial and that has grasped the enormity of circumstances which break ideas of permanence and shatter narratives. Lamentations is an antidote to denial.
- Lament can take the form of a cry for deliverance to God, which it is assumed God will hear and—it is hoped—act upon.
- Lament is the first coherent account of the kind of traumatic event that calls previously held understandings into question.
- Lament is more interested in the "how" question of immediate shock than the "why" questions of objective enquiry, but there is,

nonetheless, a theology in the background. The lamenters believe that God has allowed the tragedy to take place. They believe God must have a reason for doing so. The main reason open to human understanding at the time is sin in some form. Hence lament can contain cries of guilt alongside pleas for mercy.

Sources

At this point, we also need to say something by way of a guide to what we are reading when we read the Old Testament. That means understanding how the Old Testament came into being in the first place. We need to recall that what we call "The Old Testament" is, in fact, originally a series of documents from Judaism, for whom it is the only testament. The Hebrew Bible consists of three separate collections. The first, the Torah (or as we tend to describe it, the Pentateuch), consisting of the first five books of the Old Testament as we know it, was the first to be published, and it was the events of the Exile that appear to have prompted that publication. The Torah is an edited collection of traditions, some very ancient (in all probability, in my view, though this is contested), and some offering a contemporary "take" on the theological questions the Exile had raised. The reason we can reach this conclusion is because of the work of those scholars we call source critics, who painstakingly analysed those first five books and found ways of distinguishing between different sources for what they contain. Those different sources sometimes convey different theologies, and different responses to that traumatic event of the Exile initially reported in the book of Lamentations.

Theologies

One answer provided to the questions raised by the Exile is that contained in the book of Deuteronomy and the books describing the historical story of Israel from its creation until the Exile, comprising Joshua through to 2 Kings, as well as in some of the prophetic writings. That answer describes God's relationship with humankind in this way: "God made an agreement, called the Covenant, with a special and elect people. They did not keep their side of the bargain and got what was coming to them." At face value, that history from Joshua to 2 Kings is full of reasons why bad things happen. Disaster after disaster falls on David's dysfunctional family as a consequence of his own misdemeanours. Ahab and Jezebel come to a sticky end because of the way they treated Naboth (1 Kings 21:1-26, then 2 Kings 9:21-26), and so on. The lesson to be learned is that God's people need to keep their side of the bargain better. Penitence for the past and continuing humility are the new religious normal. This is consistent with the theology of Lamentations.

A different perspective and a different prescription are offered by a source which appears to come from a more priestly background, conveniently referred to by source critics as P to remind us of that (though again, there is scholarly discussion about the nuances contained in that "source"). The discovery prompting this alternative theological "take" was that during the Exile, the people of Judah found they could still worship God, and God could still speak to them through the prophets, *in a foreign land*. This must have come as a startling revelation. The wider culture they inhabited was one in which gods had geographical boundaries of influence; or were specific to certain situations such as warfare. Certainly, they had claimed that their God YHWH was the best God (as in the contest between YHWH and Ba'al described in 1 Kings 18, where YHWH won). But in this new international situation they came to terms with a way of thinking that was already seeded, perhaps: that YHWH was the only God. God was universal and the true author of creation. This is a key revelation and starting point for priestly theology.

To see the basis for this theology, we should read the passage Genesis 1:1-2:3, describing the creation in a careful and ordered way. Then we might look at the history contained in the books of Chronicles. They tell the same story as that in 1 and 2 Kings, but from this new and different perspective. The lessons learned in Exile are effectively emphasized throughout these writings. They stress the importance of those elements of religious observance that kept intact the religious identity (and to an extent the national identity) of Israel through the years of Exile. They included male circumcision, the keeping of the Sabbath and continuing to respect the religio-political establishment of pre-exilic times.

This theological strand is responsible for the account of male circumcision as a mark of acceptance of God's Covenant (in Genesis 17:9-14,23-27), and it is in the account of creation in Genesis 1 that we read of the importance of the Sabbath, reiterated in Exodus 16:21-30.

That account itself is the grounding for a new and creative strand in theology, based as it is on structure and ordering as being part of God's purpose. The almost liturgical repetitions of Genesis 1 are in great contrast to the alternative narrative account of creation in Genesis 2, for example. And the development of the Chronicles history through Nehemiah and Ezra describes how the idea of mirroring God's structural intentions in human society led to a view of the religious community in institutional terms. Once a view that God requires structure, order and system dominates, it will inevitably govern our view of what God is like. It says that God wants ordered lives, with boundaries respected. God wants to be approached with ordered rituals, performed by just the right people in the hierarchy performing their tasks in a ritual way. For our present purposes we note that, at face value, this institutional view of God also persuades the faithful that when something dreadful happens, it must be someone's fault (even though it deals with sin differently). God must be cross. In vast eternal plans there is always a reason for things.

We imagine the author of Job as one who is inspired by this new creation theology and who wants to explore what it means for suffering people.

Job's lament
Chapters 1 and 2 of the book are in narrative form and they set up the situation according to the worldview expressed by Shakespeare in *King Lear*, that "As flies to wanton boys are we to th' gods. They kill us for their sport."[20] There is a wager between God and (the) Satan in which Job is the unwitting and unfortunate pawn. Satan's cynical belief is that people only have a religious allegiance for what they can get out of it. Religion is essentially transactional. It's a protection racket—and if the protector fails to protect, then the whole thing will collapse, and there will be no need to pay the protection money any longer. God bets on Satan being wrong, and God arranges a series of disasters to befall Job to prove his point and win his bet. God is proved right. Even though this formerly rich man has lost his wealth, property and family, he nevertheless refuses to lose faith. He says:

> Naked I came from my mother's womb, and naked shall I return there; the LORD gave, and the LORD has taken away; blessed be the name of the LORD.'
>
> *Job 1:21*

The narrator makes it absolutely clear that Job is blameless, but also that he is not bitter, in that he does not ascribe any fault to God (1:22). He accepts the reality of suffering. Satan is not satisfied that the wager was fairly won. He believes it was only because Job did not suffer *personally* that he kept faith. Again, to prove the point God sends a dreadful disease of running sores to afflict Job. Even when his wife cannot understand why he does not simply "curse God, and die" (2:9), Job doggedly retains his integrity, saying, "'If we accept good from God, shall we not accept evil?' Throughout all this, Job did not utter one sinful word" (2:10 REB). So much for the persistence of faith.

The responsive lament is contained in Chapter 3 of the book. The "truthful" aspect of the introductory narrative is that, ridiculous though the wager in heaven may be, that is just how it feels to many who suffer, and who do so in an uncomprehending way. Yet their faith is so much more remarkable. Most of us would be with Job's wife: "Why bother? Just curse God and die." (Job 2:9); Job's response at 1:21 feels irrational. The lament connects this narrative with the rest of the book which is set in poetic form, and which records a number of exchanges between Job and three friends (later joined by a fourth). These three are representatives of aspects of the—for them—traditional religious beliefs about how and why God acts, and how we can know that.

The friends are observers as Job laments in Chapter 3. However, they are provoked to speak out of sheer indignation at what they hear him say. The lament has been described as a "literary masterpiece",[21] and consists in Job's cursing the day he was born (cf. Jeremiah 20:14–18), surely the most extreme depth to which any human can reach. The questioning typical of lament is most obvious from verse 11 onwards:

> "Why was I not stillborn,
>   why did I not perish when I came from the womb?

> Why was I ever laid on my mother's knees,
>> or put to suck at her breasts?"
>
>> *Job 3:11,12 (REB)*

Verses 13–19 give an idealized view of death, contrasting with the awfulness of life. This is notable because elsewhere in the Old Testament, death is described in very negative terms (Psalms 28:1; 30:3; 88:4,5; 143:7). Here, death is a respite in "the quiet grave" (3:13 REB). That is an expression of the depth of his grief, and sounds frighteningly close to the euphoric feelings about death admitted by those contemplating suicide. From verse 20 the questioning is extended more widely:

> Why is light given to one in misery,
>> and life to the bitter in soul,
>
>> *Job 3:20*

Verse 23 asks why man should be born to wander blindly, "hedged about by God on every side" (REB). The final verse describes why Job is making this lament: "I am not at ease, nor am I quiet; I have no rest; but trouble comes" (3:26). The word for "trouble" in the Hebrew text (*"rogez"*) is rather more suggestive of turmoil; It is the word used of the rumbling of thunder (Job 37:2), and is, dramatically, the final word of the chapter. "This is a chapter that does not pose intellectual questions concerning such matters as the reason for human suffering or divine justice, but simply exposes the rawness of Job's feelings in a way that is very rare in the Old Testament."[22] In fact, it is classic lament, presenting us with raw data and inviting us to respond to it. That response is the subject of subsequent chapters and a rehearsal of the questions raised about the religious system represented by the friends.

Job's witnesses

Job's three friends set out with the best of intentions, as the story would have it. The verb "to comfort", in Hebrew, is the same verb used of consolation in many Old Testament circumstances. It is God's word to the exiles in Isaiah 40:1, and in Psalm 23 it is the verb used to describe how God's rod and staff bring comfort and reassurance (Psalm 23:4).

However, it turns out that the use of the term here is highly ironic. What prompts the friends to a response is not their sympathy but their indignation. They had expected to hear Job's lament say at some point that it was his own fault that all this trouble had come upon him, to hear him confess his guilt and ask for God's mercy. But not once did he admit to sin. The reader knows that, in fact, Job did not sin; to the friends, however, admission of sin was the obvious and necessary first step towards restitution. That was how the world worked. That was how God worked, they believed. It is notable, however, that Job does not lose his *faithful* incomprehension. That is what creates the story. The point is, more precisely, that Job's understanding of God has been affected by his experience. He remains faithful, though uncomprehending as to quite what will take the place of the understanding of God he had, which can no longer stand. The friends are wedded to the view of God that Job has dismissed; therein lies the tension. The friends have incorporated God into a religious system, whereas Job is wondering how he can "confront the contingency of existence with the incomprehensible, transcendent God".[23] For Job, this is a God who gives and takes away, not according to a system but simply according to his will. We must let God be God, and indeed that is the theological outcome of the story.

Job's comforters cannot bear to let Job speak. They keep wanting to intervene, to justify God's actions by claiming they know God better than Job does. They know God's systems; they can speak for God. They each set out their case in extended speeches, to which Job responds. These three represent, between them, the range of possible responses that their current orthodoxy can offer. Eliphaz reminds Job of what he himself had once believed: namely that God is just, and suffering is the result of sin. "Think now, who that was innocent ever perished? Or where were the upright cut off?" (4:7). That is a fundamental, non-negotiable axiom for him. He backs that up by describing how God has spoken to him in a special vision. That strategy appears to lend authority, yet, conveniently, cannot be checked. He then goes on to treat Job to what Eliphaz has "seen for himself" (5:3 REB). In other words, he sets Job's experience against his (supposed) own. 5:17 onwards concludes his opening speech with a series of platitudes.

Bildad is the next of the friends to speak. His appeal is to tradition: "For inquire now of bygone generations, and consider what their ancestors have found;" (8:8). They thought the same as Eliphaz and Bildad, it seems. Zophar speaks last. He notes that God is silent but then goes on to say that he knows what God would say if he were to speak (11:5). None of this cuts any ice with Job. This is a wonderful parody of the compassionate response demanded by lament. Far from concentrating on Job's need, and making a comforting response, they hardly let him speak and are more anxious to preserve their own understanding, on which their vision of the world is based. They have a lot to lose if Job is right. His reply is curtly dismissive: "No doubt you are intelligent people, and when you die, wisdom will perish!" (12:2 REB).

Job 12:6, referring to the friends, can be translated as those "who bring (their) God in their hand". In other words, his complaint—in this summing-up section after the first cycle of speeches—is against those, exemplified by his comforters, who have effectively emasculated God and brought God under their control. They can bring God out of their pockets when they fancy; they can operate God to suit their own ideas of how God should behave. Job continues his argument in the next chapter: "I am ready to argue with God, while you go on smearing truth with your falsehoods . . . " (13:3,4 REB). The comforters are deeply offended. Their chief spokesman, Eliphaz, retorts:

> Should the wise answer with windy knowledge,
>   and fill themselves with the east wind?
> Should they argue in unprofitable talk,
>   or in words with which they can do no good?
> But you are doing away with the fear of God,
>   and hindering meditation before God.
>
> Job 15:2-4

Vindication and guilt

The book continues with further rounds of speeches, but then—unlike in Lamentations—we hear God speak (Job 38:1–40:2), and what God says picks up some of the imagery from the lament in Chapter 3. The setting is a tempest, wonderfully imagined by Ellen van Wolde:

> This storm is God's reaction, his answer to Job. Like a whirlwind
> he plucks up all the plans and ideas of Job and his friends, lifts
> them into the air and smashes them down again to earth. And
> after that everything is different from before.[24]

God's response is framed in a series of rhetorical questions about creation, designed to demonstrate the inadequacy and triviality of the systematic views of Job's friends. They dare to believe that they have understood the secrets of creation, but their understanding is partial and insignificant compared with the majesty of creation as God sees it. As with Lamentations, the form is part of the message. The majesty of the poetry is consonant with the vastness of creation. Again, we are presented with raw data—this time, God's raw data about creation; and through the persistent questioning of Job by God, we are invited to respond. Job's response is brief: "I knew of you before only by report, but now I see you with my own eyes" (42:5 REB). The friends' responses are judged to be blasphemous. Job is vindicated.

It is tempting to accept this as the definitive response to lament, and to dismiss others (which would involve dismissing much of the Old Testament). The book of Job does highlight a fundamental problem at the heart of being a faithful religious person, expressed by the questions, "Who speaks for God? Who truly understands God? How can we know that we have heard God's authentic voice? And how do we cope when God does answer, and says something we did not expect?"

Combining lament with confession, as if to accept unreservedly that all suffering comes from God and must be justified, leads—in my view—to two dangerous conclusions. One is about God. Do people really think that God teaches us lessons in this complicated way? I listened to one couple on a radio phone-in whose fertilization cycle, as part of a desperate attempt to have children together, had been interrupted by the recent pandemic lockdown. They said, "Why has God done this to us?" What on earth were they saying? Should the couple conclude that God didn't want them to have children, and so first he created a virus in China, then he arranged for it to come to the UK via Italy? That he then killed off a lot of people in care homes as a smokescreen before finally getting to the real point of the whole thing: their childlessness? To listen to some people lament nowadays, you might believe that this is their understanding.

The other conclusion emerges from what this kind of thinking does to us as people. It's a kind of superstition that makes us see the world as a more dangerous place, a place in which to be constantly anxious, leaving us always wondering if we have kept the rules sufficiently well to avoid dire divine consequences. Of course, we cannot and must not ignore the clear lessons of history. There are reasons why the twin towers slaughter happened on 9/11. There are reasons why the AIDS epidemic spread. But to use God either to justify or to explain one supposed causal link is a grave misrepresentation: a way in which like Job's friends, (and despite our resolute opinions), we too misunderstand God.

Responses and responsibilities

Reflecting on the theological cauldron resulting from Exile, Walter Brueggemann, in his book *Cadences of Home*, identifies six of what he calls "scriptural resources" that meet the circumstances of exile.[25] These are what he regards as potential resources to meet the effects of shattered narratives. One of these circumstances or effects he identifies is that of being orphaned. He notes the words "forgotten" and "forsaken" in Lamentations 5:20 and relates them to abandonment and rootlessness. He regards the genealogies which we find in various places in the Old Testament as a scriptural resource for that condition; they give a sense of continuity and family. "The recovery of these genealogies could indeed give an index of the mothers and fathers who have risked before us, who have hoped before us, and who continue even now to believe in us and hope for us."[26] In other words, they make us feel part of a continuum of family. Those who read the genealogies might think Brueggemann is claiming a lot for them. I have never suspected a therapeutic function for them myself, but in so far as they contribute to the whole theological strategy of order, structure and giving a community perspective to add to the liturgical one, I think he is onto something. He also picks up on the liturgical role of the so-called "Priestly writings" of the Pentateuch as another of his six resources. The circumstance he identifies in this case is the public perception of the absence of God. He believes that the sacramental emphasis to be found in those writings, allied to what we have already described (circumcision and liturgical order and the observance of Sabbath), combine to counter that sense of absence and the sense of being forgotten which Lamentations 5:20 describes.[27] Sacraments are, traditionally, occasions of God's presence.

However, it is important not to judge either of the two theological responses that we have been considering, too harshly. The "Priestly" response was, from one perspective, successful. It allowed people to move on and to feel that lessons had been learned, that a new kind of start had been made or a new stage reached in their understanding of God. That vision of an institutional model for the community of faith maintained the institution for another 400 years or so, until the destruction of the Jerusalem Temple in AD 70 caused another rethink. Alongside that, the more political and covenant-oriented theology from the authors of Deuteronomy made sure that the prophetic tradition continued in the community, reminding the faithful of their Covenant, relating judgement to actions contrary to its demand of love and faithfulness, and keeping hope alive. And we must be grateful to both for reminding us of the importance of story to identity. The fact is that human beings like solutions; we like systems that appeal to our rational sense. The evidence that God is interested in us that we want to see, we ask for in terms of order and structure. We want something we can hold God to; chaos fazes us. These are questions that naturally arise when our narratives are shattered. For Old Testament people, the Exile was a paradigmatic event of that kind. It is hardly surprising that the response of the faithful should be to try and incorporate it within a coherent narrative and a rational system, thereby domesticating it, and leaving only faithful incomprehension, rage and protest as responses.

The journey so far

So far, then, we are faced with two responses to lament. One is that God is silent, and so assumptions about God, based on human nature, fill the space left by that silence. The other is that God speaks; but says something that throws the religious world into confusion. It has misunderstood God and limited God to manageable proportions, within the boundaries of human imagination.

How do we respond to this argument in Job, and what do we learn that helps us to understand better the development of lament? We have seen:

- That lament continues to call out for compassionate response.
- That when the old sequence (people suffer—people lament—God notices and hears—God decides to act—God delivers) is interrupted and reframed (people suffer—people lament—God notices and hears—God speaks and says new things), then those new things have a bearing on how we understand the role and function of lament.
- That our understanding of the nature of lament is intimately related to our understanding of God. There is all the difference in the world between approaching God as a supplicant sinner, and approaching God as one who sees God's role as continuing to support the special project of creation, by making God's presence felt, and reminding God's people of God's continuing fidelity towards them.

Personal response

My own narrative was not so much shattered, in a Job-like way, as dismantled brick by brick, as Sue's behaviour became more and more bizarre, and the hopes that this might be something that would pass faded as the realization dawned (and as the doctors began to say) that it would never get better. It would get much worse. We all have our devastated streets, our despoiled homes, a world collapsing around us, our broken dreams. As people of faith we think God has something to do with this but we're not quite sure what, and God's silence as we lament—echoing the silence in Lamentations—means we can sometimes fill the void with ugly thoughts. We want to understand God better.

As a priest, I have visited many bereaved families in an attempt to bring the pastoral response that assures them of God's love. I have always rejected the attempt to "explain" things and, apart from when it would have been cruel to do so, have challenged the idea that this death served a purpose in God's plan: "He chooses the brightest and best to be his special angels." I have consistently assured the faithful that God did not act maliciously towards them but rather suffers with them, and have quoted Job as my reason for saying that. Job met God in his suffering.

One of the reasons that my situation with Sue could be as bearable as it was is that, although I sometimes in sheer desperation asked the question, "How?" I never asked the question, "Why?" I never hoped to find some clue from the past as to this present disaster. Whilst we had not lived entirely blameless lives, I would have had to manipulate history to an incredible degree to find a "reason" from the moral sphere as to why this should be visited on us. Of course, it was not all about me. To see it in that way would have been to wallow in self-pity and to transfer the victimhood to myself from where it properly belonged. If there were an answer to the question "Why?", I concluded that it must belong in the sphere of genetics or some other science: a pragmatic solution that could be reached with or without faith. That is not what faith meant or means to me. It was faith that persuaded me that we had actually lived a blessed life that many would envy. All human life must end, and we are never satisfied when it does. There is much to be said for Job's insistence that suffering must be accompanied by the realization of its opposite. The last thing I wanted, or thought appropriate, was pity.

Family is a place where remembering happens. In dementia of the kind Sue had, joint remembering becomes impossible very quickly. Circumstances for, and instruments of, remembering became important for me. At one level that could happen with photographs and conversations with our (grown-up) children. But at the time that all this happened, I was myself an exile, working in the Diocese of Cyprus and the Gulf, and living in Cyprus. Contact with our actual family was therefore limited, though they gave all the support they could, and of course they were suffering too. Old friends were no longer physically present, and so the congregation of which I also had oversight, St Helena's, Larnaca, became our "extended family". Liturgically, in that family, remembering happened every week in a sacramental and ordered way that I found incredibly supporting, and which I still miss terribly. In those services I remembered God and felt that God remembered Sue, me, and our family. Perhaps that's what those priestly writers were after.

I have sympathy with the priestly theologians, who sometimes get a bad press for being unintelligible and remote. I feel they have a pastoral sense; they understand the importance of structure, order and ritual. When you are a carer, those three words determine every day of your life; and when the caring has to stop, there is a huge void. The need to create new "traditions" is important, alongside other survival strategies.

Both the gathered sacramental community and the family, as well as those strategies, are markers of identity. Questions of identity are raised persistently when dementia strikes: I found myself in many conversations that seemed to assume either that Sue was now a different person or that she was no person at all. People meant it kindly. When she did something strikingly out of character, they would say—to excuse her—of course, it's not really Sue. Personhood is so often described or even defined in terms of rational cognition: I think, therefore I am; or, you are what you remember, neither of which allows personhood to a demented individual. I am convinced that personhood is a relational thing. I believe Sue remained a person because I recognized her as such and because I never ceased to love her. Within the congregation, something wonderful to see was the way that others learned to do that, rather than finding her sometimes bizarre behaviour an embarrassment. In effect they said, "Well, that's who Sue is now." Fundamentally, I believe that God also recognized her, and for the same reason. I have found the task of trying to explain faith, in the situation in which I found myself, very difficult. I value the use of symbol and poetry to help. Yes, for both of us there was a whirlwind time.

I have been luckier than Job in my pastors, but then they did not need to restrain me. I do sometimes wonder whether, after she lost the power to speak, Sue found God in her suffering. Did the tempest have a good outcome for her? I only know that one day I found a lovely holding cross that I had bought for her, made from local cypress wood by a local woodworker, snapped in two. Was this her non-verbal lament? The silence of the demented is as heavy as the silence of God. But I've stuck it together again and it's on my desk now—make of that what you will.

I am fascinated by the attempts to create survival strategies. That broken cross speaks to me about living with imperfection, making the best of brokenness, and reminds me rather of the words of playwright Dennis Potter, shortly before he died: "Religion is not the bandage but the wound."[28]

Suggestions for reflection

- Can you think of an occasion when something has happened that made you completely rethink a sincerely held belief? Perhaps it was an occasion of suffering, or something you saw or read. How difficult was it to make that change?
- Do you think it might be too easy simply to say that we've misunderstood God, and that our misunderstanding gets God off the hook? Should we regard God as jealous, angry, prone to visiting disaster after all?
- How important is the idea of family for your own identity? What is it about you that is unique and indispensable? Would you agree with theologian Dorothee Sölle that we are only indispensable to those who love us?
- Think about any experiences you have had of being the recipient of pastoral care. Do you recognize any of the traits of Job's comforters? How did you feel? Do you have sympathy with Job?

CHAPTER 3

Curlew Close

Experience

A trumpeter

Someone sent me a video of what happened on their street in Wiltshire, England, on Thursday evenings, early during the first COVID-19 crisis lockdown. It's a small, horseshoe-shaped, modern housing development that looks as if it should be called something like Curlew Close, which is how I think of it. In the video, everyone is standing outside their door, and then a cacophony of noise breaks out: the sound of banging pots and pans, shouts, applause. The occasion is brought to a close as one resident proudly brings out his trombone and plays "Amazing grace". In some ways, I guess the sound is not that different from the lamenters in Beirut, but these are not the sounds of lament. From within their locked-down prisons, people have emerged to join in a weekly ritual of thanksgiving. They want to thank those who are working in hospitals and elsewhere to preserve life, and who are taking risks with their own lives for the good of all. As well as acts of thanksgiving, these weekly rituals are acts of defiance or resistance: they say, we will not be overwhelmed. They could be said to represent the first glimpses of hope. They seem to assure us, albeit briefly at first, that in the midst of despair, in the imprisonment of desperation, a shattered narrative can be repaired. But that repair often starts in a very small way, just offering a glimpse of why life is worth living.

Nail varnish

The ability to see hope in apparently hopeless situations is most usually demonstrated, for Christians, in actions rather than in the often over-optimistic words of politicians. Just after the first Gulf War, in 1991,

Mother Teresa (1910–1997) founded an orphanage in Baghdad, under the auspices of the Sisters of Charity of Mother Teresa. I have visited the home just once, but I have an enduring memory of that visit. After the second Gulf War, in which the home survived the "shock and awe" rained upon the city, many children were orphaned and others abandoned. A chief reason for abandonment was that, as a result of pregnancies endured whilst the toxic results of warfare were a constant atmospheric presence, many children were born with abnormalities with which parents could not cope. On my visit, I saw two such young people, now teenagers. One young lady, Anoura, had been born with hands but no arms, and feet but no legs. She was bright and spoke several languages; she had learned coping strategies and for her this was her normal. Part of that normality was evidenced by the fact that she clearly fancied one of the boys, also with a birth disability. Although she had learned to cope with her physical problems, she looked a strange sight, and for a teenage girl that is obviously important. The thing that struck me, in what I can only describe as the generally relaxed and happy atmosphere of the home, was that the nuns had painted her nails. In the midst of this bombed-out city, with the abandoned and orphaned, here was one small gesture to remind everyone that this was a human being celebrating her life. She could really feel like the attractive young woman she was.

The elephant in the room

A hospice might be thought another unlikely setting in which to experience hope and vitality, yet my experience is invariably that these are places of intense statements about the importance of life, whose staff go to great lengths to do what might seem ridiculous in other circumstances in order to affirm the value of every second. Dame Cicely Saunders, who died in 2005, is the doyen of this movement in modern times, and her St Christopher's Hospice in south-east London was the template for many others. An observer writes:

> You can drop into St Christopher's as casually as you would drop into somebody's house. The restrictions are only the obvious ones of courtesy and consideration, not bureaucracy. Family pets are welcome too. A circus owner once brought a baby elephant to

see his father. No-one objected, but the elephant couldn't fit into the lift, so the sick man came down to the reception hall to see the animal.[29]

These kinds of juxtaposition are well described in a hymn by George Matheson (1842–1906), who went blind at the age of twenty, and was then deserted by the woman he hoped to marry. On the eve of his sister's wedding, some years later, as painful memories came flooding back he wrote these words:

> O Joy, that seekest me through pain,
> I cannot close my heart to thee;
> I trace the rainbow through the rain,
> And feel the promise is not vain,
> That morn shall tearless be.[30]

These examples reinforce the message of Lamentations 3:22: "The steadfast love of the LORD never ceases, his mercies never come to an end." Although this moment of optimism in Lamentations is just that—a moment—nevertheless it speaks of something that refuses to be silenced. One of the most striking things about Christianity is its refusal to let despair and fear ever completely overcome faith and hope. One of my favourite verses from the psalms of lament is Psalm 31:21: "Blessed be the Lord, for he has shown me the wonders of his love in a besieged city" (REB).

Text and commentary

Lament and praise

In the Old Testament, lament is nearly always accompanied by glimpses of faithful hope. The prophet Jeremiah's name is synonymous with lamentation, to the extent that editors thought it natural to reposition the book Lamentations next to his. Yet tucked away in the middle of the fifty-two chapters of his book is a four-chapter section sometimes called "The Book of Consolation" or "The Book of Comfort" (Jeremiah

30–33). "Beyond the judgments that have taken place, therefore, the Book of Jeremiah asserts categorically that hope remained real."[31] This section cloaks that hope in a vision of a restored Israel, back within its own geographical borders and party to a new covenant (Jeremiah 31:31; 33:6–9,19–22). Although new, this description of covenant is a way of relating the past to the present and declaring God to be faithful throughout. In other words, this is not just a *prediction*: it is a *prophecy*, and as such bears witness to the nature of the God of Israel in terms of divine fidelity. It is a mantra moment: a time to call to mind the axioms of faithful relationship.

We see the same juxtapositions within the psalms of lament. Claus Westermann's definitive study, *Praise and Lament in the Psalms*, describes how praise has a definite place in psalms of lament. These fragments of praise in the midst of lament have what he calls three motifs. The first is the one in which the lamenting community remembers and makes reference to God's saving deeds in the past. Psalm 44 is usually designated a "communal lament" or "the lament of the people"; the lament proper begins at verse 9—"Yet you have rejected and abased us"—and continues to its "rough" address in verse 23: "Rouse yourself! Lord, why do you sleep? Awake! Do not cast us off for ever. Why do you hide your face? Why do you forget our affliction and oppression?" Yet the psalm had begun with a recollection of God's great deeds in the past (Psalm 44:1–8), which is essentially what brings faith to incomprehension. Other similar examples would be Psalms 85:1–3 and 106:8–11.

Then there is praise that is a confession of trust, and which comes at a point in the psalm between the lament proper and the petition (the prayer to God for rescue from distress). Psalm 60 gets straight to the heart of the matter: "O God, you have rejected us, broken our defences; you have been angry; now restore us!", and there follows the evidence for that claim. But then at verse 5 we have the confession of trust that God is capable of acting: "Give victory with your right hand, and answer us, so that those whom you love may be rescued." And this leads into the prayer, "[G]rant us help against the foe . . . " (60:11). Lamentations 5:19 could be read in that way. In the midst of pathetic lament, there is a final appeal: "But you, O LORD, reign for ever; your throne endures to all generations." This leads into the final prayer to be restored and renewed. Similar examples can be found elsewhere in the prophetic writings. Jeremiah 14 begins by telling us that Judah "droops" and that her towns "languish", but concludes, "Is it not in you, Lord our God, that we put our hope?" (Jeremiah 14:22 REB).

The third kind of occurrence is where a vow of praise is made linked to a promise, an oracle of salvation, an *a posteriori* burst of praise. Psalm 79 begins with a description of Jerusalem in ruins and the temple defiled; birds feed on corpses. There follows a lengthy petition—a "to do" list for God. The final verse contains a description of the praise that will come to God after he has acted: "Then we your people, the flock of your pasture, will give thanks to you for ever; from generation to generation we will recount your praise." (Psalm 79:13). "Here therefore within a Psalm, lamentation is often turned into praise."[32] The most interesting examples are those in which a prophetic oracle is assumed to have been given within the body of the psalm, so completely changing its nature. "This explains the 'abrupt change of mood' [citing Gunkel] from lament to jubilation within a Psalm."[33] A clear example is found in Psalm 22, the Psalm found on Jesus' lips on the cross, which begins, "My God, my God, why have you forsaken me?" This psalm has been described as "the principal Old Testament resource employed by the evangelists to portray, and so interpret, the climax of Jesus' career".[34] Other verses from Psalm 22 are also quoted in the Gospels (Mark 15:29; Matthew 27:39, 27:43; John 19:28; Mark 15:24; Matthew 27:35; Luke 23:34; John 19:24); these Gospel occurrences are cited following their order in the psalm, and all come from the first twenty-one verses, which contain the initial lament. But at verse 22 there is a completely new theme: "I will tell of your name to my brothers and sisters; in the midst of the congregation I will praise you:" The conclusion is that what "happened" liturgically, after verse 21, was the reading or declaration of a prophetic oracle (similar to that at Jeremiah 30:10), which completely changed everything. God had responded. There was hope.

The psychology of formation

In *The Message of the Psalms*, Walter Brueggemann discerns a bigger pattern of psychological movement in the Psalms, which he describes as taking place in three stages. These could be taken as stages in human understanding and mature religious formation. The entry level he describes as "Psalms of Orientation".³⁵ These are psalms appropriate to a situation we might think of as the old normal, the blue remembered hills, the age of lost content, this being a time when the only real response to a world understood and experienced as firmly ordered, just and trustworthy was praise and thanksgiving. The second stage he describes as "Psalms of Disorientation". These, consisting mostly of the laments, describe the shock of discovering and experiencing the various representations of evil and corruption in the world. A third movement he describes as that towards what he calls "Psalms of New Orientation", which demonstrate that healing has happened, a new normal has been realized and a more mature worldview accepted. Sometimes all three stages can be discerned within a single psalm: Psalm 30 is a good example. Here we see, first, the easy unquestioning assurance (v. 6), then the circumstances of despair (v. 7); the words of the lamenting prayer follow (vv. 8–10), and then the immediate response, "You have turned my laments into dancing" (v. 11 REB), followed by the continuing praise (vv. 1–5,12). That is the complete three-stage movement.³⁶

Although the movement from despair to hope and lament to dancing is chronicled by individuals and communities in a condensed and liturgical way in the Psalms, the book which has as its major theme a message to exiles, to break into their despair with hope, is the book we might call Deutero-Isaiah (or Second Isaiah).

Deutero-Isaiah

This is a "book" that you will not find in any Bible's table of contents. It consists of one portion of the book taking its name from the prophet Isaiah. It is widely accepted by scholars that the book of Isaiah, as we have it, is an interreferenced compilation of works from three separate periods, following a consistent theology. Deutero-Isaiah consists primarily of Chapters 40 to 55 in our Bibles.

The story of Isaiah begins in the eighth century BCE in Jerusalem, but with Deutero-Isaiah we skip a couple of hundred years to somewhere around 540 BCE. At this time, the Israelites are still experiencing the Exile in Babylon, whose beginnings, with the sack of Jerusalem, are described in Lamentations. Deutero-Isaiah speaks from their midst. Of course, very few, if any of those addressed would have been original exiles. They would have been second- or third-generation exiles, with a cultural memory of belonging elsewhere but having become accustomed to living in Babylon. In the year 539, the Babylonian Empire fell to the Persians. At their head was Cyrus, first mentioned in Isaiah 41:25: a military hero who had already defeated the legendary king Croesus of Lydia in 546. The political writing is obviously on the wall, but Deutero-Isaiah interprets all this as an act of God, preparing the exiles for imminent freedom. The attitude of Cyrus to conquered nations was different from that of the Babylonians. He encouraged local management and the development of indigenous cultures, as opposed to the laying waste of conquered lands favoured by the Babylonian Nebuchadnezzar. Consequently, Isaiah's prophecy soon proved correct and the Israelite descendants were given permission to go home if they wished. The books of Ezra and Nehemiah describe the exploits of those who did. Isaiah reflects that strand of religious belief which regards the fate of Jerusalem as crucial. His message is that God has remained faithful and promises have been fulfilled. God has a distinct and contemporary message for his people in exile.

The text begins with the prophet being asked to speak tenderly. This is a kindly word, and it is a word of comfort in two ways. First, it draws a line under the past; that is now forgiven, though none of the usual Hebrew words for forgiveness are used, possibly because communal forgiveness is a relatively novel concept. (We should not forget that forgiveness is much more a New Testament than an Old Testament concept.) Second, God is doing a new thing: on God's initiative the past has been transformed. In fact, monotheism really comes into its own in this book. God is truly international, able even to organize the affairs of foreign kings such as Cyrus (Isaiah 45:1–7). God is not only the creator of the world; God is organizer, creator, and designer of human history, and specifically, creator of Israel. Creation theology has met liberation theology. Within this majestic picture, reminiscent in its rhetoric of sections of the book of Job, are embedded four passages which have been identified as "songs of the suffering servant", and they give us a particular insight into the theological creativity linking despair with hope and lamentable suffering with praise.

Servant songs: vocation and redemption

The first passage is 42:1–9, and here we begin to encounter something quite paradoxical. On the one hand, there are lofty descriptions of God as the only God, creator of all things. On the other, we are introduced to God's servant who has a hefty vocation—to establish justice among the nations (42:1), to open the eyes of the blind and release captives from prison (42:7)—but whose nature is gentle, careful and considerate. The vocation is reiterated in the second poem, 49:1–6, where we hear the voice of the servant and then God's response. The servant is here addressed as Israel, but his vocation is not just concerned with Israel. God's vision and ambition are much greater: "I will give you as a light to the nations, that my salvation may reach to the end of the earth."

The third song is 50:4–9. Whereas in the first song the servant is empowered by the Spirit of God (42:1), here the servant is empowered by God directly, his call comparable with that of the call of the major prophets (49:2), enabled for him by listening to God (50:4,5). This is what has given him the power to withstand the abuse he suffers (50:6). This is the first indication we have that the servant, by being empowered in this way to withstand suffering and abuse, can be an empowering example to others. Paul Hanson, reflecting on the role and character of this figure, says this:

> It is one of the mysteries of life that those with the greatest ability to encourage the distraught are often people who, far from being exempt from suffering, discover special gifts of empathy and empowerment precisely in their own valleys of personal suffering.[37]

The link between suffering, vocation and compassion is made in an interesting way by the writer Harry Williams. He equates despair with isolation, taking the wilderness as a metaphor for that isolation in which we are tempted to cynicism, cruelty or outright despair. However, he regards this as a necessary part, or a necessary stage, of our formation as human beings. He takes heart from Mark's account of the temptations of Jesus: "He too did time in the wilderness. And what happened to Him there shows us what is happening to ourselves."[38] He notes that the same

Spirit which sent Jesus to the wilderness had, immediately beforehand, "brought Him the conviction of being called to do great things".[39] But angels ministered to him; in the "wilderness of despond" he found, through the ministry of angels, a reason to go on to claim his vocation.

The most famous and longest of the servant songs is Isaiah 52:13–53:12. This poem was eagerly seized upon by the first Christian apologists as they tried to find a way of interpreting the death of Jesus in order to locate hope and faith, in the midst of the narrative-shattering event of the crucifixion. Its echoes are to be found throughout the New Testament.[40] In this poem the servant's suffering is enlarged upon, but crucially it is described as not without purpose or achievement:

> But he was wounded for our transgressions, crushed for our iniquities; upon him was the punishment that made us whole, and by his bruises we are healed.
>
> *Isaiah 53:5*

The servant so described was passive. He let all this happen to him, but God vindicated him.

Yet the Lord took thought for his oppressed servant, and healed him who had given himself as a sacrifice for sin (53:10 REB); he had borne the sin of many and interceded for transgressors (53:12).

This is a complex message. It maintains the idea of God's initiative but stops short of saying that God caused the servant's suffering. The responsibility for that appears to rest with his tormentors. There is a two-fold redemption here—the suffering of the servant is for a purpose: it redeems the sins of many. But his suffering is also redeemed by God and transformed into vindication. The described demeanour of the servant is striking—there is nothing triumphalist about him. What he is to achieve, he will achieve without force. This is a powerful message to suffering people, both in terms of its gentleness and in terms of its vocation for them. Though suffering, yet they have a purpose, a vocation, and their suffering means and achieves something. Alongside this is pastoral assurance, which we see clearly in a new idiom in Isaiah 41:8–13 and 43:1–7. The gospel message, "Do not be afraid", occurs no less than six times. There is an intimacy to these passages: "I take you by the right hand;" (41:13); "I have called you by your name. You are mine." (43:1); "You are more precious to me than the Assyrians, and I love you." (43:4).

As a result of political circumstances, which can be attributed to God's intervention through the eyes of faith, the people can return to the ruined Jerusalem and rebuild it, as the books of Nehemiah and Ezra record. The "prediction" can be realized. But it seems that few wanted to return. The community addressed was only suffering in a theoretical sense: they were not those who had experienced the long march; they were not those who had endured the early days of slavery. Many had become place-makers of the kind envisaged in Jeremiah 29:4–7. Hanson believes it would be more precise to describe Deutero-Isaiah's strategy as rescuing the community from cynicism and religious despair, perhaps with those in mind who have been tempted to give up on YHWH and to try out other gods (Jeremiah 44:16–18).[41] Robert Carroll develops this theme. He believes Deutero-Isaiah is an example of "dissonance resolution"—in other words, a continual reinterpretation of a promise not fulfilled.[42] Therefore, they needed not only to be consoled but also to be inspired, and undoubtedly the rhetoric of Deutero-Isaiah is amongst the loftiest in the Bible. The argument is that God both has a plan and has the means of accomplishing it, so they should trust him to restore order from chaos and establish a new narrative (46:10). But the idea that suffering can set an example or be redemptive—that is, that it can achieve a greater good—is, theologically speaking, perhaps the most striking message in this text. It describes one way of finding hope and maintaining faith; one way of recognizing God's continuing care and compassion, and crucially a way of finding meaning in suffering. God has a job to be done. Those who have experienced suffering can do it best. The suffering now is for a good purpose and a good outcome.

The idea of redemption in this sense of redeeming a situation (which is, in fact, its most frequent modern usage) really begins with the story of Joseph and his brothers. The story starts at Genesis 37 and concludes with Genesis 50. Apart from a short interjection at Genesis 38, this is a continuous narrative in which Jacob's son Joseph becomes a victim of his brothers' jealousy, to the extent that first they plot to kill him, but then sell him into slavery instead. As a result of this infamy, Joseph is taken to Egypt, where an entertaining series of events sees him become prime minister with responsibility for what turns out to be a successful plan for the nation to survive an impending famine. Eventually, the truth about their crime finds its way out and Joseph's brothers come to ask his forgiveness. Joseph says to them:

> "Do not be afraid. Am I in the place of God? You meant to do me harm; but God meant to bring good out of it by preserving the lives of many people, as we see today. Do not be afraid. I shall provide for you and your dependants." Thus he comforted them and set their minds at rest.
>
> *Genesis 50:19–21 (REB)*

This passage describes the possibility of redemption in a way that will, in the future, provide one rational answer to the problem of suffering, as we begin to see in Deutero-Isaiah. It describes redemption as an initiative of God and relates redemption to forgiveness, in the context of that repeated gospel word of reassurance, "Do not be afraid." It describes a God whose purpose in intervening is to make things better. It is a comforting word. Whatever other powers God may or may not have, the power to redeem is certainly one of them. Redemption, on this evidence, could be described as God's being faced with a bad situation, and on his own initiative, with a pastoral intention turning it to good purpose.

Caring

The passage combines these motifs with that of comfort. Joseph comforted his distraught brothers. In recent years, many Christians have become accustomed to singing the Taizé chant "Ubi caritas et amor; ubi caritas Deus ibi est", translated as, "Where there is charity and love, God is to be found." There are few more potent signs of God's presence than what the Old Testament describes as "*hesed*", usually translated as "lovingkindness". If we are looking for an intervention by God, and if we are trying to hear God's voice, discern God's presence, or see evidence of God's redemption, then loving care seems to be a good place to start. As the message of Isaiah continues in its third phase, the author summarizes much of what has gone before:

> I will recount the *hesed* of the LORD,
> the praiseworthy acts of the LORD,
> because of all that the LORD has done for us,
> and the great favour to the house of Israel
> that he has shown them according to his mercy,
> according to the abundance of his *hesed*
>
> *Isaiah 63:7*

Loving care reminds us of the best in us, and of better times, and that whatever else has been destroyed, the potential for that kind of care persists and is at the heart of Christian vocation. That is precisely what is so scary about Lamentations. It describes a loveless situation. Human relations are brutal; gentleness, tenderness and the comfort that they bring are completely absent. Even maternal love—an expression of the ultimate in love, in human terms—is no longer evident.

A poem by the Christian songwriter and poet Sydney Carter captures the sense of how such a situation can be redeemed. Entitled "Mother Teresa", it describes a situation of utter hopelessness, different from that in Baghdad, in which she intervenes. This is a reflection on her work in Calcutta, concentrating on the plight of one poor man who has only twelve more hours to live:

> No revolution will come in time
> to alter this man's life
> except the one surprise of being loved.

The poem goes on to describe in tender detail the way she ministers to him, a way that Carter describes as showing "dangerous love". It concludes:

> But if love cannot do it, then I see
> no future for this dying man or me.
> So blow the world to glory,
> crack the clock. Let love be dangerous.[43]

That very same comfort can be found, not only in Deutero-Isaiah's initial announcement (42:1), but also especially in Isaiah 43:1–14, with its combination of words expressing redemption and the gospel message, "Do not be afraid." One of the drivers of hopelessness is that we find ourselves unable to see a way out of the situation we are in, let alone a strategy for taking that way. What is described in the Old Testament as an oracle of salvation, breaking into our despair, could perhaps be thought of today as seeing the hand of God in an intervention we had not anticipated. Or, to put it another way, reviving our sense of miracle.

I am happy to see the hand of God in events, and to hear God's word in commentary on those events. A famous poem by the modern Welsh poet Gillian Clarke expresses something of what I mean. It describes a true event in which she, as a poet, is giving some extramural therapy to residents of a care home for the mentally ill by reading poetry to them. It is March, and the daffodils are in bloom. Verse 2 begins starkly, "I am reading poetry to the insane". There are examples from the "congregation" to back up the claim. Then the poem centres on one "big, mild man". This man is led to his chair. He has never spoken; his world is completely closed. He listens to the poems, gently rocking, and then:

> He is suddenly standing, silently,
> huge and mild, but I feel afraid. Like slow
> movement of spring water or the first bird
> of the year in the breaking darkness,
> the labourer's voice recites 'The Daffodils'.[44]

The poem goes on in wonder to imagine how the man first learned that poem by heart in some "Valleys school". Everyone applauds. It is an unthinkable moment. Everything has changed, both for her and him, and for the group. She calls the poem, "Miracle on St David's Day". That speaks to me of a modern sense of miracle, when looking back we can say, "Who would have ever thought . . . " Maintaining a sense of miracle is, I think, a means of experiencing an exit from despair. These interventions in our ordinary life are perhaps equivalent to those brief interventions in lament when the clouds part to reveal a reminder of God's presence.

The journey continues

In this chapter, we have considered the role of what look like awkwardly juxtaposed bursts of praise, optimism and faith within lament, and within the exiled community which was also responsible for some psalms of lament (most noticeably Psalm 137). The key words and ideas that have resulted are these:

- *Comfort* is what lamenting people crave from their silent God. When God speaks, the word of God is a word of comfort. The primary authentic response to lament is a compassionate one.
- The Psalms play a part in describing human *formation*, the journey towards discovering what it is to be truly human. Lament can be said to describe a stage on that journey.
- Within that framework, lament may be the voice of individuals and communities vocalizing a *vocation*.
- That vocation can be as agents of *redemption*, that is, a way of turning a negative experience to positive good.
- The unexpected *interventions* into the Psalms and elsewhere mirror the way God's interventions are made into ordinary, experienced life, in a way we sometimes describe as "miracle".

Personal reflection

In early December 2018, I slipped and fell outside our house in Cyprus, breaking my hip. I had to spend several days in hospital before returning home. I think that during the whole period of Sue's illness, this was the only time that I was acutely aware of needing comfort. Of course, I was well looked after in hospital, and during that time we had a nursing agency looking after Sue at home. Our son was able to come out and take the strain immediately after my discharge. We had established a pattern of having people in to sit with Sue only when I was not at home, and I wanted to continue to do that. After our son left, I continued to look after Sue on my own. It is not easy to carry hot food walking gingerly with a walker, and in pain. Sue did not like the walker and thought the best way for it no longer to be needed was to throw it across the room if she got the chance, wondering why I had to crawl after it on my hands and knees. I remember being in despair then. I was really low, and felt I had no resources left. I suppose you could say I needed above all to feel empowered again, but I never really lost hope that I would be. That is the power of mantras!

Christmas Day that year was especially bad. I could drive—I had first done so just over a week after I had been discharged. Sue loved going for a drive in the car. It calmed her, and it was an essential survival skill for me to master again quickly. On Christmas Day, we went to St Helena's Church, where I celebrated and preached, hobbling up the aisle with my walker and sitting down more than usual, but I found that very tiring and had little energy left by the time we got home. Our Christmas dinner of bacon and egg was eaten in a house devoid of decorations, with no cards (since Sue usually tried to tear them up if she saw them). Presents were opened with no sense of pleasure whatever. It was the lowest point on a day that should have been one of the high points of the year. I felt truly alone. But then, out of the blue, I had a phone call from Veronika, the young woman who had been Sue's principal carer until she needed more specific nursing care from people used to the unpredictable and sometimes violent behaviour of dementia sufferers. She asked if it would be all right if she and her fiancé came round to spend the afternoon with us. And was there anything they could do, and would Sue perhaps like to have a short trip out in the car? Oh yes! Comfort has never been more comforting.

That was to be Sue's last Christmas. On our return to Wales, the social and medical services decided it was going to be best for Sue to go to an assessment unit, prior to finding her a suitable place in a home. I had known this would happen one day, but it still came as a shock. I knew I should never share a bed with her again after forty-eight years of doing so. I would never have the chance to really care for her again. I was handing her over to other people who didn't know her, and I was in despair. This time our daughter shared that burden. However, when I saw the unit to which Sue was admitted and the incredible commitment of the nurses who worked there—their gentleness and understanding—and saw how she began to make a relationship with them, speaking to them with her eyes, I was reassured. In both cases, my despair turned to hope as a result of having experienced genuine, one might say, loving care, *hesed*. The situation had been redeemed.

Isolation is well described as a wilderness—a place of individual and silent lament. Any kind of depressive illness tends to a gradual shrinking of our world's boundaries, and indeed an increasing focus on ourselves alone. We become self-centred. During the COVID-19 crisis, we have all been encouraged to stay apart, leading to a situation which may finally prove difficult to escape from, in which my neighbour is seen as my enemy, and we treat all people with suspicion. The sense of isolation this brings is an engine of grief. Readmission to society, a new appreciation of the role of community, a vision that gives us a place—and what we might even call a vocation—in a bigger picture, is what we need to respond to that grief. Modern-day carers will immediately recognize this condition of isolation; what social life you had disappears. That is partly due to time constraints, but also to the fact that you are no longer fun to be with, particularly if you are caring for someone who it is difficult for a visitor to be with: someone who doesn't speak and looks at you in a slightly scary way, and leaves you with a sense of having done your duty rather than having had a good social time together. Going to someone's house for a meal loses something if one of you has to hand-feed another, who keeps regurgitating the food on to the plate; or if the meal you, as host, have carefully and thoughtfully prepared with the dementia sufferer's needs in mind is rejected with the words, "I don't like this".

This is what caring is actually about from day to day when someone like Sue, whilst still able to do some things but not others, is clearly unwell. My congregation at St Helena's, Larnaca, to whom this book is partly dedicated, were absolutely fantastic, like ministering angels in the wilderness, as was Veronika (the other dedication) on a day-to-day basis. Some people valiantly continued to welcome us to their homes, and the congregation as a whole responded in every way they could to make Sue feel part, still, of a loving community. They had seen the journey week by week; they were, as the hymn says, fellow travellers on a journey. But perhaps more than that. Perhaps her being a member of the community had helped everyone to recognize their true vocation as a community, and helped our corporate progress in formation. In my final sermon there, I spoke of how Sue's illness and all that it involved had, I thought, made me both a better priest and a better person, and I think that struck a chord.

Back in the 1980s and 1990s, I used to devise and present religious programmes for HTV Wales, and in that capacity I once had the privilege of interviewing Dame Cicely Saunders. I asked her what she considered to be the antidote to death. Without hesitation she answered that the antidote to death is community. I found that puzzling at the time, but understand it better now. The Bible has many antidotes to isolation, ranging from the concept of vocation to the presentation of a cosmic vision in which we can be excited about our part, to the whole idea of the church as the compassionate family or the people of God. Like modern carers, when that caring looked like ceasing, the people of Israel needed a narrative for re-entry. Deutero-Isaiah provided that for them and it is no accident, I think, that at its heart stands that gospel message: "Do not be afraid for I shall be with you."

Suggestions for reflection

- Can you think of a time when hope has "broken into despair" and when you have had a sudden insight into what really matters? How important was that insight in seeing you through your experience?
- Can you think of an experience of redemption in your own life? Have you seen the 1994 film *The Shawshank Redemption*? Why do you think that title was chosen?
- Put yourself in the place of someone who has become a bit cynical about religion. Would reading Deutero-Isaiah help to change your outlook?
- Can you think of a formative time in your life when suffering or hardship helped to make you a better person?
- Can you think of an example of "miracle"?
- Have you ever felt alone, perhaps even beyond a point when you can articulate lament? Did you find a community to be drawn into? Do they understand the part they played?

CHAPTER 4

Bosnia

Experience

In the mid 1990s I was part of a team making a TV documentary about the work of Army chaplains. Because we were a Welsh station, we were concentrating on one particular chaplain who was Welsh, telling part of the story through him. This involved our going to Bosnia, where he was stationed at the time, with a scattering of other journalists—organized by the Army's PR department—on an RAF flight. The fighting had just ended, and the evidence of its destruction was everywhere. On my return on the rattling old Hercules plane, I found myself sitting next to a young television journalist. We were all swapping accounts of different places we had been to and people we had seen. She wanted to talk about an experience she'd had which had clearly shaken her. She had been taken to a town where there had been a sizeable Muslim minority, and had interviewed a Muslim survivor. He had described, with great sadness, how he had managed to escape a round-up of a few Muslim families by some local militia. These Muslims, including women and children, had been told to stand underneath a bridge. Then they blew up the bridge on top of them. She said that in telling the story, the man had paused at that point and then said, almost wistfully, "I know the man who did this. He was my neighbour." The journalist said that for the first time she had really appreciated what was meant by evil.

Intifada memories
In 1989 I was part of an ecumenical delegation to Israel and the West Bank (as we then described it), which spent time with both Israeli and Palestinian communities. This was the time of the first so-called Intifada

and tensions were high. We visited one clinic in a Palestinian village where we heard accounts of brutality. Pregnant women showed us the marks where they had been beaten. We heard of a practice, outlawed as illegal by the UN but widespread in Israel at that time, in which, as a punishment for some relatively minor infringement (such as children throwing stones at tanks), a family was ordered to remove all their furniture from their home. And then the home was blown up, often on top of their furniture. It filled us with horror. During that visit we met many people who were lamenting in the same way that the Old Testament victims had done. One paragraph from the report we subsequently published describes both the brutality and the contrasting signs of hope that so characterize biblical lament, and which we noted in the last chapter:

> At the Ahli Arab Hospital in Gaza, founded by the CMS, and now under the direction of the Anglican Diocese of Jerusalem, we met a doctor who is well-known in Britain for her previous work in the Lebanese refugee camps. She had been removing bullets from the day's Palestinian casualties—three dead and twelve injured. Outside, the signs of defiance were everywhere—burning tyres billowed out black smoke. Yet in the distance a child was flying his home-made kite, and the hospital was celebrating the birth of three boys.[45]

Chaos and restoration

These examples from Bosnia and Palestine both echo the witness of Lamentations. They describe the breakdown of common understandings about boundaries: about what was considered natural or inviolate and about dignities that must be preserved and had been all but abandoned. If unborn children could be put at risk with this brutality, if homes were not considered sacred but could be wantonly and intentionally destroyed along with the treasured possessions that told a story and gave an identity, if neighbourliness ceased to have any currency, what hope was there for humankind? In Lamentations, we see examples of the complete breakdown of society. Women "eat their offspring" (Lamentations 2:20). Dreadful tortures are devised, as described in Lamentations 3:53, "they flung me alive into a pit and hurled stones on me;" and this was done by "those who were my enemies without cause" (3:52). There is no food, even for children (4:4). It is every man for himself; the order of society has been turned upside down (Lamentations 5:8).

This is the breakdown of social structure. The horror, in all these cases, was not just the immediate suffering and hardship caused—summed up in the phrase "man's inhumanity to man"—but something much deeper. It was a horror that civilization itself was unravelling. What is shocking and unnerving about these accounts, as they bear witness to the breakdown of normal society, is how easily people can normalize brutality rather than neighbourliness and cooperation. They mark that shift in human formation, as we saw outlined by Brueggemann in the last chapter, from orientation to disorientation. He describes the shift briefly thus:

> This move is experienced partly as changed circumstance, but it is much more a personal awareness and acknowledgement of the changed circumstance. This may be an abrupt or a slowly dawning acknowledgement. It constitutes a dismantling of the old, known world and a relinquishment of safe, reliable confidence in God's good creation. The movement of dismantling includes a rush of negatives, including rage, resentment, guilt, shame, isolation, despair, hatred and hostility.

He goes on to say, "The lament is a candid, even if unwilling, embrace of a new situation of chaos, now devoid of the coherence that marks God's good creation."[46]

In this chapter, we shall consider biblical material that recognizes that chaos, and is concerned to restore God's good creation. It will do so, not so much by a politically inspired demand for conformity to the terms of the Covenant between God and the nation of Israel, but rather by an insistence that restoring broken relationships will require a new level of holiness among the people of Israel. This material is associated with the religious establishment, the priests. It is less well-known than the writings associated with the authors of Deuteronomy and the majority of the prophets, which tend to dominate the Old Testament as a whole. Their social and political account has much more attractive and memorable passages and stories than that of priests, whose contributions to the Old

Testament can seem remote, dense and inaccessible by comparison. Nevertheless, it represents a response to lament—and the causes of lament—which sees a role for the community of faith, in a way that might make it more useful in determining how today's community of faith can hold and use the tradition of lament, as a community of honest sadness.

Text and commentary

Ezekiel

The prophet Ezekiel experienced the Exile at first hand. He was almost certainly among the first deportees to Babylon in 597, and his prophecy covers the period that includes the final sacking of Jerusalem in 586. Some of his oracles are specifically dated, and they range between 592 and 570. For him, Jerusalem's significance was not tied to his family or domestic securities, but rather to his priestly belief that God had his dwelling there, in the temple, in a special way. He was not the only person to feel this, and the priests were probably speaking for the whole nation, but as a priest, Ezekiel felt this particularly acutely: "[T]here can be little or no doubt that the rank and file of those who were carried away into Babylon felt that they were not only leaving their old home and their kindred, but also their God."[47] The lament in Psalm 74 centres on the destruction of the temple and "every holy place throughout the land". God no longer has anywhere to dwell, and there are no prophets left to speak for God (Psalm 74:8,9). For Ezekiel, Jerusalem is the dwelling of "the glory of God", and his concern is for God's reputation, especially among the nations; his assessment—and the content of his judgement on Jerusalem—was that it had become contaminated, and needed to be purified.

The judgements he delivers are contained in the first half of the book, Chapters 1 to 24. They are often expressed in bizarre or lurid images, some of which have been described as pornographic. This has led to a major critical focus on the prophet's state of mind: he has been diagnosed with every psychological state known to humankind, and this has cast some doubt on the authenticity of his account. More recently, however, theologian Daniel Smith-Christopher, using insights from anthropology and refugee studies, has examined the evidence and reached a different conclusion. He believes that Ezekiel was suffering from post-traumatic stress disorder, which could well have been brought on by the very experiences whose aftermath we see described in Lamentations. In other words, the weirdness of the visions authenticates them.[48] Moreover, from evidence in modern refugee studies that accepting that "we deserved it" is a coping strategy for lamenting people, Smith-Christopher believes the most lurid of the judgements may have exactly that purpose.[49] He matches Ezekiel's descriptions with those in Lamentations to authenticate them further.[50]

The picture Ezekiel paints of God is terrifying, and accords with the worst descriptions of Lamentations:

> "Go through the city of Jerusalem," said the Lord, "and mark with a cross the foreheads of those who groan and lament over all the abominations practised there." To the others I heard him say, "Follow him through the city and deal out death; show no pity; spare no-one. Kill and destroy men old and young, girls, little children, and women, but touch no one who bears the mark. Begin at my sanctuary."
>
> *Ezekiel 9:4–6 (REB)*

In Chapter 10, the "glory of the Lord" leaves the temple; God has gone (10:18). There follows a whole sequence of judgements, including a judgement on religious life which, in Ezekiel's view, has to take some responsibility and reform itself:

> Its priests have done violence to my teaching and have profaned my holy things; they have made no distinction between the holy and the common, neither have they taught the difference between the unclean and the clean, and they have disregarded my sabbaths, so that I am profaned among them.
>
> *Ezekiel 22:26*

In Chapter 24, Ezekiel's wife dies. Although recognizing that she is "the dearest thing you have", God tells Ezekiel that he is to show no sign of mourning, and his action is to be taken as a symbol—a metaphor for God's loss of his sanctuary. At 33:21, the word eventually comes to the exiles (via a fugitive from Jerusalem) that the city has finally fallen. This is a turning point in the book as the focus now changes to restoration (Chapters 33 to 48). In a perverse way, considering the matching violence and aggression of the language and images in Ezekiel and Lamentations, perhaps it is as well that, in the latter, God does not speak. Ezekiel tells us what God might have been thought to say in those circumstances; this is an austere and loveless God, quite uncharacteristic of the Old Testament description more generally.

Ezekiel makes much of the image of the unfaithful woman, the whore. In Chapter 23, he equates Jerusalem with a woman he calls Oholibah, giving an extended account of her prostituting herself with Chaldeans, Egyptians, Assyrians—anyone who would have her (23:11–21). This is really uncomfortable reading. The image of the whore is utilized elsewhere in the Old Testament to denote the breaking of a faithful relationship, but in a way that expresses the accepting love of God.

God as husband

The most affecting account is that in Hosea, where the relationship between God and his people is also set against the human experience of a marriage. The prophet Hosea's dysfunctional marriage in which he continues to love his prostitute wife Gomer, despite everything she does, provides a quite heart-rending metaphor for God's longing for his people. We hear in Hosea 2:13 that she "decked herself with her ring and jewellery, and went after her lovers, and forgot me, says the LORD". But now God intends to take her back to the place where the romance began: the wilderness. Translations are rather coy about what happens next; the *Revised English Bible* says he will "woo her", as does NRSV. The *New Jerusalem Bible* says he will "seduce her". The most obvious meaning, in comparison with Genesis 34:3, is that he will make love to her again as only a husband can (Hosea 2:14). Alongside this is another tender relationship image—that of a father and son:

> When Israel was a child, I loved him,
> and out of Egypt I called my son.... it was I
> who taught Ephraim to walk,
> I took them up in my arms; but they did not know that I
> healed them. I led them with cords of human kindness,
> with bands of love. I was to them like those
> who lift infants to their cheeks. I bent down to them and fed them.
>
> *Hosea 11:1,3,4*

The comparison with Ezekiel's view of God is stark: we are left with the suspicion that Ezekiel has been brutalized by his experience. But this is not a judgement on him—this is how life seems to its victims, just as Job's suffering logically links to a capricious and uncaring God. We long even more for an authentic voice of God; we want to hear God speak for Godself.

Making a new start: Noah

So how do the more considered priestly writers deal with the move from chaos to a new normal? Priestly theology takes its cue from the account of the creation of the world in Genesis 1. Creation is described there in an almost liturgical way, stressing the boundaries between different species, but stressing also their interdependence and connectedness. Unlike the (traditionally) earlier account of creation which we find in Genesis 2, the priestly understanding is that humankind (in both sexes) comes, finally, into an already existent environment and is charged with stewarding it. The order of this chapter presents a template for order throughout the whole creation, based on the number seven, while the content sets out a worldview that manages to put both relationship and boundaries centre stage. But this is a hopeful theology.

We saw it reach its heights of hopefulness in Deutero-Isaiah, and Deutero-Isaiah connects us, conveniently, to the story of Noah: "This is like the days of Noah to me: Just as I swore that the waters of Noah would never again go over the earth, so I have sworn that I will not be angry with you and will not rebuke you." (Isaiah 54:9). As the final editors of the collection of books we call the Pentateuch, the first five books of the Old Testament, the Priestly theologians were the people who told the story of the flood in its final form, combining their own theological ideas with an older tradition. It is interesting to think of them telling the story of the flood, in the context of the complete breakdown of society as represented by Lamentations, with the theological hopefulness represented by Deutero-Isaiah. And perhaps that is the best way to understand the story of the flood: not as an ancient myth from the mists of pre-antiquity, but as the basis of a response to the experience which Lamentations describes, and which we ourselves can recognize.

The Priestly account of the flood has an outcome summarized in Genesis 9:1–17; but it takes its cue from Genesis 5:29, where we are introduced to Noah and hear an explanation of his name. The name "Noah" means "rest", and is related to a root meaning comfort or respite. The verse is sometimes translated into English in a way that suggests the respite is from work (for example REB: "this boy will bring us relief from our work"; or NRSV "this one shall bring us relief from our work and from the toil of our hands") but that is probably not the original intention. What Noah will do is to bring respite by redeeming the cursed earth. Noah is essentially God's second shot at creation. The first attempt went disastrously wrong: Adam and Eve were disobedient, Cain killed Abel as a first example of the violence that was to develop (6:13), and earlier in Chapter 6 we hear about the complete breakdown of the created order (Genesis 6:1–4). God recognizes that his every good intention in creation has been subverted and "the LORD was sorry that he had made humankind on the earth, and it grieved him to his heart." (Genesis 6:6; cf. Jeremiah 3:19,20). This amounts to God's lament and is the first such example, of which many will follow (e.g. Jeremiah 2:2–37; Hosea 11:1–9; Amos 6:1–8; Micah 1:8–16). These passages are often classed together as oracles of judgement, and indeed they are—but then the people's laments are also expressing judgement on God. Lament is a vehicle for both sides of a broken relationship. However, Noah appears as a new comforter in the midst of God's lament.

"Noah is to do for humanity just what Second Isaiah announced for Israel then in exile... These connections are not remote."[51] In the Genesis account, the story is placed in the context of the wider question posed in the first eleven chapters of the book, namely, "Will God's good creation be subverted, inevitably, by human evil and sinfulness? Or will that human evil and sinfulness be overcome by God's grace?"[52] That is the central and fundamental question in the Bible. In that context, God does not give up on humankind as he had been inclined to do (Genesis 6:7), but rather "remembers" Noah and decides on a new strategy. Quite startlingly, that strategy is that God will live with human imperfection and maintain the grace he first demonstrated in creation (8:21). In other words, God's response is not to find a way by which "this can never happen again", but rather to have a survival and coping strategy recognizing the fact that inevitably it *will*. The extent of the new offer is huge. It is a promise "never again" to put the earth under a curse because of humankind (8:21). The slight revision of the original scheme of creation in Genesis 9:1-6 has the effect of strengthening respect for life, and human life in particular. The lamenters have been "remembered", heard, answered.

The new normal

Effectively, then, the tension will continue between God's grace and human nature, and that is part of what we might call "the new normal". In a sense, expectations on both sides of the God/human relationship have had to be reined in. God has accepted the reality of sin. Humankind has to accept what, from a human perspective, look like limitations on God's power, or at least God's intention to use it. The continuity with the initial intentions in creation is maintained by the repeated use of the phrase, "Go forth and multiply" (Genesis 1:27,28 and 9:1,7). Those initial intentions for human life remain. And the whole deal is marked with a new and final statement of the Covenant—the agreement that describes the relationship between humankind (no longer just Israel) and God. The Covenant is the standard point of reference throughout the Old Testament for the developing and varying understandings of the relationship between God and humans. For example, the promises that Ezekiel describes in Chapters 33 to 37 are as dramatic as what has gone before, but the nub of the promises is a restatement of the Covenant (36:24-28). A new covenant will signal a line drawn and a new beginning.

The theme of making a fresh start with a renewed relationship is a common one in post-exilic writing. The authors of Deuteronomy—the first to grasp the implications of monotheism that exile had prompted—make a distinctive contribution to the understanding of covenant:

> Previously we had a covenant consisting of the ordinary commands of an ordinary god upon an ordinary henotheistic (more or less) people. After Deuteronomy, we have a Covenant consisting of the special commands of the Only God upon a people specially chosen by Him.[53]

The Genesis 9 Covenant, from the Priestly theological school, is the most universal of all. It applies to all creation, without political mediation. From now on, there is no need for the whole of creation to live in anxiety. The future of creation has been underwritten. In Genesis 9, this is presented as an act of God's grace; there is no demand in return. God has accepted living with a new normal in which disasters will happen, as a result of human nature being what it is, but despite that, he makes his offer of life.

Mending relationships

The key element in this covenant relationship was "*hesed*" (see, for example, Genesis 24:27,49; 47:29; Exodus 34:6; Deuteronomy 7:9,12; Joshua 2:14; Jeremiah 9:24; Hosea 2:19; Zechariah 7:9). This Hebrew word is usually translated "loving-kindness", but in a classic study, Norman Snaith makes the case that this is not strong enough and not in keeping with the word's etymology, which derives from the idea of eagerness and steadfastness. He translates *hesed* as "covenant-love", but that doesn't tell us much apart from the idea being a technical term associated with the Covenant; it is also associated with words for truth, mercy, compassion and righteousness. Snaith argues that this is an unfailing and persistent love: "The most important of all the distinctive ideas of the Old Testament is God's steady and extraordinary persistence in continuing to love wayward Israel in spite of Israel's insistent waywardness."[54]

Throughout the Bible, reflections about "what went wrong" inevitably refer to broken relationships, and reflections about "what we should do" inevitably focus on repairing them. Although this may not be as evident in the New Testament, by a simple comparison of the number of times the word "covenant" appears (some 240 times in the Old Testament, around two dozen in the New), we should nevertheless remember that "Testament" is itself an English translation of the Greek word for covenant. The New Testament could equally well be called, in its entirety, the New Covenant. We should also remember that God demonstrates his relationship not only by the act of incarnation itself, but also by calling disciples and forming trusting relationships with them, setting a pattern for the community of faith in the new dispensation. Christians will be those in a relationship with Christ. Faith is a relationship word, like trust and love; the opposite of faith is not doubt, but fear. For "new normal" read "new covenant".

Having to adapt to a new normal is a common experience following a narrative-shattering trauma. Refugees have to adapt to life in a new country with a strange language and different cultural expectations. After 9/11, travellers had to get used to new procedures in airports and elsewhere, with new security checks. After the economic meltdown in 2008, many people had to get used to new regulations about buying houses or banking. In the various pandemics of the twenty-first century, it has become commonplace in some countries for people to wear face masks as a matter of course. In some of those cases, the new arrangements are part of a control mechanism to counter a threat. In others, the concept of risk analysis has new significance.

Perhaps the most challenging are "new normals" at the personal level. Coming to terms with a new disability means a new sense of being different from everyone else, and new coping strategies have to be learned. The experience of bereavement is one of those changes most common to all. Pastors will recognize that a new normal for people whose whole focus has been on caring for the person who has died, and whose whole pattern of life has been dictated by the vicissitudes of their illness, have a particularly difficult time of it. The important message from Genesis 9, though, is this: that dystopia is not the only alternative to utopia. There is a pragmatic compromise possible; that is what makes the "new normal" new. It is notable that God's ratification of the new normal, his giving of a blessing and his solemn promise, happens in response to—or as a consequence of—Noah building an altar and offering sacrifices of ritually clean animals. This is a theological marker for the Priestly sacramental theology, finding practical detailed description in the book Leviticus, which has been described as an extended commentary on Genesis 1.[55]

Leviticus

The first half of the book is addressed primarily to priests, though laity have their responsibilities. It contains ten "liturgical commandments" in two groups of five: the first five concern sacrifice and the second five purity, as conceived at that time (dealing with things like skin disease and bodily discharge). The underlying idea is that creation itself has been corrupted and contaminated. The ritual of Leviticus is meant to mirror God's creative intention, and so is often based on a series of seven. Genesis 1 is the blueprint, so the number seven has special significance—not only because it signifies the whole of creation, but also because the seventh day is "God's day". The authors believed that following a sequence of seven would lead to a greater understanding and appreciation of God's presence, and would also set out a view of a perfect world, such as God intended. The ritual acts aim to get rid of all that stands in the way of the realization of this perfect, holy, pure world. The rituals also put a framework of order around creation. They believed that God created intentionally, with definite divisions and boundaries. These divine intentions were to be respected in the political and social world as well; ignoring the divisions had been part of the problem that had brought chaos. There is a negative side to this, as seen (for example) in the development of the apartheid systems in various places in the world, though given that name specifically in South Africa. But it also has modern resonance in a more positive way. Disasters nowadays often provoke a response from those modern environmentalists that the Priestly theologians would have seen as fellow travellers. Viruses move from animal species to humans because we are too careless of those boundaries. We are too ready to despoil the environment for short-term economic gain, they tell us. The disaster at Aberfan in the Welsh Valleys in 1966 was the result of just such environmental carelessness: 144 people died, mostly children, when a colliery spoil tip moved and engulfed a school. As noted in the Preface, I cannot think of lament without referring to it. The anxiety caused by such careless or malign human intervention is the stuff of which Stephen King novels are made.

Leviticus 17 to 27 are addressed mostly to the laity (with the exception of Chapters 21 and 22). They concern holiness, and the section is sometimes called "the holiness code". In this code every aspect of life is examined, and instruction given concerning it; all of this is meant to mirror God's holiness and God's order. The vision set out is not wholly unattractive. Chapter 19 deals with social justice and issues of community cohesion in quite a modern fashion. Here we learn that the poor and the alien should be able to eat freely of what remains after a first reaping of crops, the so-called gleanings. It is wrong to withhold wages. Blind and deaf people must be respected and cared for. The neighbour's need is to be counted as one's own. We see here also the Priestly obsession with boundaries and the maintenance of purity. Cross-breeding is not allowed. Two kinds of seed should not be sown in a field. Clothes made from two types of cloth should not be worn. All of this is in homage to the idea that humankind is made in God's image, and so any defilement creates a wrong image of God: God's reputation is at stake. The ritual and behaviour are no longer, as in olden days, meant to appease God. Ritual and behaviour are redefined to focus entirely on God's holiness.

One radical consequence is the belief that economic life must also follow order and pattern. Belongings and ownership must not be asserted, because the earth is the Lord's and we are God's tenants (Leviticus 25:23). In Chapter 25 we see that agriculture must follow a pattern of sevens. Every seven years the land must have a "sabbath rest". Every fifty years (seven times seven, followed by a jubilee year) there is to be no cropping; food will be eaten direct from the field. In that year, all land will revert to the "original owner". When one buys a field, one is not buying property, but buying the number of crops until the next jubilee (25:15). The field remains God's. He is the freeholder; we are the leaseholders. This is a complete, radical vision of a new kind of society based on creation theology. There is some doubt as to whether it was ever totally adopted, but this is the tradition that informed Judaism going forward after the Exile from the time of Ezra. This is a vision that ascribes responsibility for the Exile, not in political terms (as the Deuteronomy theology does, blaming poor leadership), but rather in terms of the defilement of God's creative intention. To restore that is to set a new track. Peace in the future will be based on a joint honouring of creation and justice, and this will be the substance of the latest form of the Covenant. The land which was cursed has been redeemed; now blessing is the order of the day. A great deal of lamentation is concerned with cursing. At some point this has to turn to blessing, if life is to be grasped.

This tradition is properly called sacramental, because of the way it rehearses God's presence through ritual. As Brueggemann says, "It is important to us, in our exilic situation, to renotice that these texts constitute a major pastoral response to the exilic crisis of absence."[56] Lamentations is notable for the absence of God's voice, and the cries of the faithful who feel abandoned; God seems either distant or absent altogether. Through sacramental acts in a specially designated holy tabernacle, God's presence can be remembered and perhaps "felt". Brueggemann goes on, "I suspect that for exiles, a verbal presence by itself is too thin, which is why the Priestly materials came to dominate the canon."[57] This, then, is a successful strategy incorporated in a new covenant. Notably, in Hebrew, Leviticus is not given a name which smacks of institutionalism, but rather, following the opening words of the book, its name is "God Calls". Almost bizarrely, this book will take its place among the other unlikely contenders, such as Lamentations and cursing psalms, in the holy and sacred traditions and memory of the Christian faith.

The journey continues

- In this chapter, we have seen the fragility of social cohesion, the chaos, anger and vulnerability that result from its breakdown, and the fear that this should be normalized, expressed initially in lament.
- We have seen the startling new initiative of God, which accepts human sin in a new normal.
- We have noted that the restoration and repair of social cohesion is regarded first as a theological issue. Relations with God must be restored.
- The evidence for this is a new Covenant, once again as God's initiative, huge in its scope.

- We have seen how the religious community—represented by the writing priests—approached the problem, with an innovative creation theology that laid new responsibilities on earth-dwellers.
- We have also seen how they devised rituals: dramatic representations of the intimate communion between God and humankind, designed to restore and inculcate holiness and purity, maintain boundaries and give assurance of God's presence to cleanse and heal.

Personal reflection

I am haunted by the picture of this abusing, merciless God who Ezekiel believes is speaking through him. Smith-Christopher may be right, that it is what the people want to hear so that they can retain a sense of order and meaning. But that is precisely why I think it is wrong. To say that suffering is caused by sin, on this scale or a much more personal one, means that it can easily be dealt with: all you need is forgiveness. And that reduces religion once more to a predictable system. I think a better paradigm is the one that again I find shocking in its expression in Ezekiel, namely the marriage relationship, which is ideally based on grace, not law. What I find most shocking there is that, in order to make a point, God is represented as refusing Ezekiel (clearly a devoted husband) the right to a proper funeral for his wife. Perhaps that's what pushed him over the edge. It has had a documented effect on those who, throughout the COVID-19 pandemic, were unable to give their loved ones the funeral they wanted. Funerals are satisfying and mark a first stage of resolution. In Wales in particular, in my experience, they have a dignity and formal framework, comparable with the poetic metre in Lamentations, allowing a full expression of both grief and thanksgiving.

That is not by any means to say that there is no more grieving to do. Many people have attempted to console me in my recent bereavement by pointing to the fact that I have lots of work to do "to keep me busy; to take my mind off it". And they are right to a point—I do have work to do and I am lucky in that respect. But what they do not always realize is that from time to time I see little point any more in doing it. My sense of purpose in life died with Sue, at least for a time. She had been my centre of meaning. My understanding of my relationship with God was tied up with that relationship in a complex way. It is very easy to be dismissive about life in those circumstances. And so I have to undertake the task of finding a new centre or centres of meaning which can carry that weight. "God is; he is for me; so it is worth it." is a mantra that I desperately need to keep repeating while I find that centre.

A poem by Robert Frost (1874–1963) helped me to focus, a famous one called "Stopping by Woods on a Snowy Evening". Some people think this is a poem about contemplating suicide; gladly, that interpretation has not reflected my own feelings. I see it, like other Frost poems, as about making choices, and being committed to the choice made. The poem is set on "The darkest evening of the year". Someone making a journey by horse is at a point nowhere near a village, a place without landmarks, when he stops. The reader is made to feel uneasy—an uneasiness represented by the horse in the poem—"My little horse must think it queer/To stop without a farmhouse near". There are two points in the landscape that take the rider's, and so the reader's, attention. One is the snow which we imagine both as a bright white carpet but also as a possible obstacle to travel; the other is the dark wood. The poem ends with the traveller making his choice between them, reiterating his resolve by repeating the final line of the final verse.

> The woods are lovely, dark and deep,
> But I have promises to keep,
> And miles to go before I sleep,
> And miles to go before I sleep.[58]

What speaks to me in this poem is something I have always known without realizing. Hope and purpose are based on being a party to a promise—a covenant, if you like. What I have come to realize as well is that to keep my side of the promise actually enables others to have hope. Hope is fuelled by promises. At one level, God has made promises to me, and I in return have made promises to God in liturgical settings and prayers and thousands of Eucharists. But the promise became most real in the promise that stood at the heart of my life: my marriage to Sue. I think that is why faithfulness is such a big deal in the Bible, and why the image of the whore and the adulterer is so powerful in describing the betrayal of faithfulness. I think of the people to whom my promises count: my incredible family, close friends, people whose lives have changed as a result of things I have told them about God. Hosea was quite right to put relationship at the heart of life. A new normal, if it is to be hopeful, should be couched in terms of renewed relationship. That is not just true at the personal level: economic life depends on the promises found on every bank note; international peace depends on treaties signed in good faith. It is the loving community that is best placed to resist all that dehumanizes and corrupts life. Communities of honest sadness must reflect that.

I am fascinated by the inclusion of the texts we have seen so far in the collection of Christianity's holy books, and so given an importance in the corporate memory. Lament has played an important part, not just in the process of individual formation, but in the communal understanding of theology which represents the corporate evidence of formation. And the sacramental tradition, with its beginnings in creation theology, has resonance for me too. In any deep relationship, be it marriage or the relationship with God, the sacramental acts associated with them continue to make each of them real, immediate, important and, in their own way, vocationally inspiring.

Suggestions for reflection

- What evidence might you draw on from your experience of "civilization unravelling"? What kind of emotions do you experience as you think about that possibility? Anger? Fear? Regret? Hopelessness? Or something else?
- Think of the story of Noah as you may recognize it in popular culture. Does the interpretation offered here bring a new perspective? What changes as a result?
- Has someone ever betrayed the faith you placed in them? What scars did that leave? What would count as healing?
- Read Ezekiel 23, which is basically an allegorical description of Near Eastern politics over the previous couple of centuries when

the author was writing. How easy would you find it to say, "This is the word of the Lord." afterwards? Do you believe that?
- Can you think of a relationship of which you are a part which features "*hesed*"? How important is that to you?

CHAPTER 5

Baghdad

Experience

Question time

One of the devastated cities of recent times that lies within our Diocese of Cyprus and the Gulf is the city of Baghdad. My first visit there was in 2011. I remember it well because it coincided with a service in the American Embassy there, to mark the tenth anniversary of the twin towers disaster, at which I preached and celebrated. The main event at our church of St George was to be the ordination of our first indigenous Iraqi priest. When senior diocesan staff visit Baghdad, there is usually a programme arranged to make the most of their presence, and so it was in this case. On the evening we arrived, a few of us had been asked to form a "Question Time"-sort of panel for the young people of the church. Arriving in Baghdad was a stressful thing at that time. With the offer of a bulletproof vest, you were driven from the airport at breakneck speed with horns and sirens blazing, threading amongst the traffic with a pickup full of armed guards in front and behind you. When I arrived at the church compound, I felt lucky to be alive, if I'm honest! It's not something that ministry in Pembrokeshire prepares you for. They said there had been a drive-by shooting that had killed four compound security staff relatively recently, and the previous year 144 people had been killed by a massive explosion within the grounds, with explosives packed into a cement mixer. Armed security staff accompanied us everywhere within the compound, on the lookout for snipers from the collapsed and ruined buildings all around us. It was the landscape of Lamentations.

Good news

In this unpromising wasteland, the church operated—and still does—in a heroic way. Apart from the congregation of some hundreds each week, there are three clinics, an early-years school and an extensive food programme which is a lifeline for local people. Travel at that time was very difficult, and you never knew how many people would be able to get to church events. But on that first night we faced around forty young people, aged between about fourteen and twenty-five. And as it happened, I was the first to answer the opening question. A girl in her mid-teens put the question (in Arabic, and translated as was the response), which was this: "What can you tell us that will give us hope?"

That was a question which haunted me throughout the visit, and especially during the ordination itself as the new priest was given a Bible and commissioned to preach the gospel. What, I wondered, was God's good news to people here? The young woman's question was heartfelt and real. It came from a context of faithful incomprehension, a bit like a combination of two verses from Lamentations: "Then I cry out that my strength is gone and so has my hope in the Lord" (3:18 REB), and the "but yet" of 3:24— "The Lord . . . is all that I have, therefore I shall wait for him patiently" (REB).

I wonder how we would answer that young person's question. I have come to believe that we often use terms like "preaching the gospel" almost as slogans, without thinking about what we're really saying. If I were to ask a representative group of Christians (if such a body could be found), "Could you describe the gospel to me? What is the good news from God that we want to persuade others to hear and believe and accept? Is there a hymn that says it all, for example?", I would not be surprised to get a response along the lines of, "He died that we might be forgiven, He died to make us good; that we might go at last to heaven, saved by His precious blood." Although that's an old hymn now, it has many modern equivalents. So is that what I should have said to my Iraqi girl in the midst of her hopelessness? She who had experienced years of war, who had seen one of the most civilized and sophisticated cultures of the Middle East reduced to Stone Age proportions, penury and violent sectarianism with no prospect of worthwhile work, family security or peace—should I have said, "Well, at least I have some good news: your sins are forgiven."?

Or even, "You'll go at last to heaven—it'll be OK when you die."? And if that sounds too much of a caricature, should I have taken the line of an American military chaplain who had produced a video presentation to precede my commemorative Eucharist at the embassy? Over pictures of the devastation of 9/11, a country and western-style gospel singer sang a song which had a chorus that went something like this: "I'm just a regular guy; I don't really know the difference between Iraq and Iran" (pronounced "eye-raq and eye-ran"); "but this I know—Jesus loves me." Is that our gospel? Is that God's good news? To those experiencing the silence of God, is that what God might have said to them?

The gospel is not a one-size-fits-all commodity to be marketed: it is one half of a conversation of which we are privileged to be part. The Bible—and not just the New Testament—abounds with good news to different people in different situations: good news about health and healing, about the security of creation, about a God who constantly urges us not to be afraid because God is with us. There is good news that evil has been conquered; there is good news that life has a purpose, and we have a destiny. And going back to our hymns—yes, there is good news about forgiveness, and that is especially good news for those struggling under a burden of guilt. And yes, there is good news about being loved by God, and that is especially good news for those who have never experienced human love, or who suffer from low self-esteem, but that is not everyone all of the time. We have to listen in our conversation to the things that have caused people to lose faith, to the news they long for. And we have to listen to the range of good news the Bible offers in response. That is surely part of what it means to be witnesses.

The soup kitchen
I have already mentioned my filming visit to the Balkans for a documentary about Army chaplains. On arrival at Split airport, we received a lecture on the five ways we were most likely to die during our stay, and then we were driven—wearing our bulletproof vests—to an Army establishment at a place called Kupres, high in the mountains: a former ski resort that had been on the front line during the war which had recently ended. This was another devastated town. One day we accompanied the chaplain on a welfare mission, driving through the minefields to a neighbouring town

within a Serb enclave which looked even worse. We were taking some resources for a soup kitchen run by the Salvation Army. It was bitterly cold, there was no power in the homes, the buildings were in ruins, the people looked thoroughly miserable. We learned that the children of the families using the soup kitchen had learned a song in English that they were going to sing especially for us. I recognized it as a modern worship song, familiar to the Salvation Army volunteers who were running this little welfare centre. It began, "Our God is so great, so strong and so mighty, there's nothing that he cannot do." Listening to the small children singing, while trying not very successfully to fight back my tears, I don't think I have ever been more aware of a bitter irony. This place had been devastated by armies, each of which believed the sentiments of that song for their own side: Catholic, Orthodox, Muslim. Whatever the strength and power of God might mean, it surely could not mean something that could result in this misery, this legacy of death and hardship.

Text and commentary

Forgiveness and power

One way of interpreting God's silence in the face of lament is to believe that he has nothing to say because there's nothing he can do. Mark's Gospel, by common scholarly consent the first to be written, assumes that the good news people want to hear is about the power of God. One of the themes of the New Testament more generally is that people must rethink the power of God. We must always recall that the Gospels were themselves written from an initial context of despair: people who had hoped for great things from a powerful God in human form had seen him crucified. As the likely ending of Mark's Gospel says, the first disciples had no idea how to respond to this new situation, and its aftermath in the Easter garden, that called for such a radical rethink. "They said nothing to anyone, for they were afraid." (Mark 16:8). Mark begins his Gospel, then, with assertions about Jesus' power, interpreted in terms of authority.

The public ministry of Jesus begins in Mark with several acts of authority that are linked to his teaching (Mark 1:27). The demons speak loudly but Jesus silences them (1:25,34). Then the first extended account of public ministry comes in Chapter 2. This describes the healing of a paralysed man brought by four friends to Jesus. In a story known by all who ever attended Sunday School, they are unable to get near Jesus because of the crowds, so they let their friend down on a stretcher through the roof. Those details of the story help us to imagine a theatre of high drama with lots of spectators. The incident is important because it describes Jesus' authority in terms of his power to forgive. Not only can he silence demons, but he can also forgive sins. This is the controversial claim that provokes the questioning scribes (Mark 2:6,7). The function of this story is not to make a connection between sin and illness, so defending the conservative belief that illness must be deserved, that it must be a punishment for something—the doctrine that Job challenged—but rather to give evidence of the authority of Jesus. No-one can "see" that sins have been forgiven. There needs to be a demonstration. The fact that the paralysed man could walk confirms that claim.

It is interesting to note that there are surprisingly few instances of God's forgiveness in the Old Testament. God is described as a forgiving God in Exodus 34:7 (cf. Numbers 14:18–20), but these occurrences seem quite ambiguous. Alongside describing God as forgiving, they go on to say, "forgiving iniquity and transgression and sin, yet by no means clearing the guilty, but visiting the iniquity of the parents upon the children and the children's children, to the third and the fourth generation" (Exodus 34:7). What kind of forgiveness is that? It is certainly at odds with what Jesus describes. Of the other occurrences, many are contained in prayers, describing a desire for forgiveness but no evidence of it happening (2 Kings 5:18; 2 Chronicles 6:21–39). The late post-exilic author of Nehemiah, associated with a priestly school who have confidence in rituals for getting rid of sin (e.g. Leviticus 16:20–22), cites the fact that God did not abandon his people for their disobedience in the Exodus, as evidence of God's forgiveness. Deutero-Isaiah begins with an affirmation that Israel is now pardoned, in the sense that she has paid the price demanded (Isaiah 40:1,2).

According to biblical scholar Donald Gowan, forgiveness is primarily part of the eschatological expectation of the Old Testament.[59] The city of Jerusalem is often used as an image for this expectation. That, in turn, is linked to the situation described in Lamentations: to the experience of exile and the sense that certain fundamental things must change if restoration of the ruined city is ever to take place. It is not enough to think of forgiveness in terms of one human forgiving another (difficult as that often is), or for human initiatives and institutions to form systems that ensure judicial process or arbitration. It is not enough for humans to devise a religious system for dealing with sin, such as the priestly initiatives to restore the world's holiness through cultic ritual (see Leviticus 1–7). That is a limited understanding of forgiveness, though it is how most people experience it. What is needed, rather, in the bigger scheme of things is an initiative on God's part to offer what Gowan calls eschatological forgiveness:

> The fall of Jerusalem and the exile so impressed those who were left alive with the certainty that they had fallen under God's judgement for a longstanding and thoroughgoing series of acts of rebellion against him, that they understood that only an unprecedented, gracious act of forgiveness could make possible any future for them as the people of God. And so almost every text that we here deal with concerns the exile.[60]

One response to the experience of lamenting is the assurance that the new start can be made, the slate wiped clean, no baggage carried forward. Forgiveness is possible. And so the novel focus on forgiveness in the New Testament has a quite specific reference. It is an antidote to lament; it gives new significance to the power of God being shown in forgiveness. We can see the hope expressed clearly as early as the eighth-century prophet Micah. He has his own lament about the state of things in *his* time. The prevalent social norms are abandoned, with evidence of social chaos:

> Put no trust in a neighbour,
> no confidence in a close friend.
> Seal your lips even from your wife whom you love.
> Son maligns father,
> daughter rebels against mother,
> daughter-in-law against mother-in-law,
> and a person's enemies are found under his own roof.
>
> *Micah 7:5,6 (REB)*

In his prayer and vision of restoration he affirms, "He will again have compassion upon us: he will tread our iniquities under foot. You will cast all our sins into the depths of the sea" (Micah 7:19).

The hope of forgiveness, in the sense of drawing a line under history and making a fresh start, is at the heart of the New Testament proclamation of the Kingdom of God. Baptism is a mark of entry into that kingdom, or at least readiness for it, by acknowledging sin washed away (Mark 1:4,5). In the Matthean version of the Last Supper, as Jesus asks his disciples to remember him in bread and wine, he specifically mentions that the wine represents blood shed for the remission of sins, and that it is shed for many (Matthew 26:28).

Forgiveness and healing

There is a separate question about whether illness is related to sin. Another account of a healing miracle, this time in John's Gospel, tackles the issue of whether moral misdemeanour has physical consequences such as illness. In John 9, Jesus sees a man who has been blind from birth. His disciples ask him, "Rabbi, why was this man born blind? Who sinned, this man or his parents?" (John 9:2 REB). Jesus' answer says something quite profound about both God's justice and God's power. "It is not that he or his parents sinned," Jesus answered. "He was born blind so that God's power might be displayed in curing him" (9:3 REB). In other words, the disciples asked the wrong question about God's justice. The issue of how he came to be blind had nothing to do with God. It was simply a given. Indeed, the whole story, which takes up virtually the entire chapter, is about how the facts on the ground need to be accepted at face value, rather than being treated as if they were to be interpreted in terms of some vast eternal (and mistaken) plan. The demonstration of the power of Jesus to heal is one such fact. The Pharisees cannot accept what is plainly obvious, because it does not fit the logic of their religious system. Their understanding runs something like this: "Healing comes from God. This man cannot come from God because he does not keep the Sabbath. Therefore he is sinful and cannot do anything on God's behalf. Moreover, he bypasses the one sure authority which is that of being disciples of Moses." (John 9:16,28). The man who is cured points out that they are looking through the wrong end of the telescope. They should start with experience: "This man can heal; therefore he must be from God." But the passage also says something important about God's power, which Mark's story also shows. It is demonstrated not in the power to punish but in the power to forgive. This is an endorsement of the tentative word of faith we heard in Lamentations 3:22, that God does not willingly afflict.

An interesting passage which only appears in Luke's Gospel confirms that view. This passage is Luke 13:1–5, and it occurs at a point in the story when Jesus is making the long journey from the Sea of Galilee to Jerusalem and using that as an opportunity to teach at various places along the way, some of which are significant (in Samaria, for example). Some tragic news has reached this place: Pilate has assassinated some Herodians (supporters of a political movement from the north). This is described in gory detail: Pilate "mixed their blood with their sacrifices" (Luke 13:1 REB). That sentence also suggests that they were going about religious business when they were killed. There is always something more remarkable when people are killed in a religious setting, when they appear vulnerable, and where that vulnerability is contrasted with violence. In the original *Godfather* film, the sequence of killing at the end is all the more dramatic because it is contrasted and interplayed with a baptism service. But having recalled the scandal of the Herodian massacre in Luke's account, we might imagine some hecklers shouting, "And what about the Siloam Eighteen!" Clearly this was a notorious case, as the remembrance of the exact number of deaths is mentioned; we know no other details of this fatal incident. Jesus tells them it was a tragic accident: "Do you imagine that they were more guilty than all the other people living in Jerusalem?" (Luke 13:4 REB). Tragic accidents are not to be confused with acts of God. However, Jesus adds a kind of "Let this be a warning to you." comment. Everyone needs to repent for eschatological forgiveness to be experienced.

The forgiving community

One additional point about the relation of forgiveness to lament concerns what forgiveness demands. It is sometimes assumed that the main responsibility arising from receiving forgiveness is to sin no more, based perhaps on the words we read in our Bibles at John 8:11. That, of course, is impossible for humankind. As Paul says, try as he might, he finds that despite himself he still sins (Romans 7:14-20). The Gospel imperative to those who are forgiven is rather that they forgive others. This is at the heart of the Lord's Prayer; it is also a major theme of the wider "Sermon on the Mount" (Matthew 5:23,24; 6:12,14,15). Whereas sinning no more emphasizes the individual as an individual, forgiving others emphasizes the role of a person in relation to other people. It is a community thing. Other references to forgiveness in the Gospels are clearly designed to be part of showing how members of the church community relate to each other (Matthew 18:18; John 20:23). Or to put it another way, churches are actually meant to be communities of the forgiving—of those aware of having been forgiven. Their discipline needs to be built on that base. It is still the case that none can forgive sins except God alone. Others can only do so in his name, with the assurance born of narratives such as the one provided by the fragment above that has found its way into John's Gospel, describing the woman taken in adultery (John 7:53-8:11). Hence we learn that lamenting communities, going forward, must not only be communities of honest sadness. They must be communities of realistic forgiveness. Forgiveness is one way in which the power of God is displayed.

Power and redemption
So far, we have identified the power of God as the power to forgive. The New Testament is also the place to pick up the suggestions we saw in Deutero-Isaiah, that God has power to redeem. Much New Testament imagery on this theme is taken from the fourth servant song in Deutero-Isaiah (Chapter 53). New Testament scholar Barnabas Lindars writes:

> Although actual quotations from this famous chapter are not specially numerous in the New Testament, allusions to it are embedded so deeply in the work of all the principal writers that it is certain that it belongs to the earliest thought of the primitive Church. It is highly probable that it was inherited from Jesus himself, and that it exercised a decisive influence on his mind.[61]

Leaving aside this last opinion, certainly this was a key passage for those trying to make sense of a God who could be crucified. Mark 10:45 is often cited as one important place where it surfaces: "For the Son of Man did not come to be served but to serve, and to give his life as a ransom for many." This word "ransom" has much to answer for in subsequent theology. Over the centuries, scholars have worked out complicated schemes and theories on the basis of it, trying to describe "atonement"—that is, what God accomplished on the cross.

The Church is not just the community of those who will forgive; it is also a community with redemption at its heart. I hesitate to call it the community of the redeemed, because that seems to suggest something insular and exclusive, a community of the holier-than-thou, which is the exact opposite of what I believe is intended. The Church must be a community whose vocation is to forgive and redeem, continuing the work of Christ and using the tools of humility, love and sacrifice that he used. This is a vocation well summed up by the author of Hebrews: "Therefore Jesus also suffered outside the city gate in order to sanctify the people by his own blood. Let us then go to him outside the camp and bear the abuse he endured." (Hebrews 13:12,13). Redemption, vocation and forgiveness are closely related, as in the servant songs. In fact, if we turn to the Gospel of Matthew, we see "push-back" against any idea that the Church is an elite community. In Matthew 13:24–43, we read the parable of the wheat and the tares: a corrective to those who believe that the community should be perfectionist and internally judgemental. Any community that is judgemental towards its own members will certainly be judgemental towards others. Matthew's church is to be a mixed body. It will have a definite disciplinary code (Matthew 18:15–17), based on attempted reconciliation. It has a vocation towards the "least".

In the Gospels, God speaks, through Jesus, for himself, to lamenters. God demonstrates power, not in the way that the lamenters intended, but in forgiveness, healing and redemption. God achieves redemption not through might and coercive power, but by being servant-like and suffering; and in the person of Jesus, God proclaims good news. We read in Luke 4:18,19, of Jesus announcing his ministry priorities by quoting Trito-Isaiah, a later prophet still, responsible for Chapters 56 to 66 of the Old Testament book Isaiah, who picks up the themes of his predecessor. The mission is to announce good news to the poor, and specifically to proclaim release for prisoners and "broken victims" (the Greek word has the original meaning of "to break in pieces"). We could equally translate it with almost any word describing the human condition which has the prefix "broken": broken-hearted, broken-spirited, for example. Perhaps simply "the broken" captures the sense. They are the ones who lament.

Apocalyptic: God in control
However, it must be said that within the Gospels there is evidence of another tradition altogether: it has a different view of God's power, sees redemption as a final victory over the powers of evil, and has little to say about forgiveness. That is the tradition of apocalyptic. In the first three Gospels it appears at Mark 13, Matthew 24 and Luke 21; the latter two are clearly dependant on Mark, but all three strike a slightly discordant note in their context. In Mark, for example, this long soliloquy from Jesus is a style not used elsewhere in the Gospel. But the discordance is more pronounced than that. It is generally referred to as "the little apocalypse", because it exhibits features both stylistic and theological that belong to a particular genre of religious writing, and which is thought to be a distinct and discrete source for Mark which he has incorporated in its entirety. In the New Testament, examples of apocalyptic writing are found here in the Gospels and also in the book of Revelation (its name being the English translation of the Greek word "*apokalypsis*"). There are allusions to it elsewhere. It is interesting when considering lament because, as a genre, it derives from *situations* of lament. Writer S. B. Frost believed that it was conceived as a response to the "How long?" of the Psalms, and was indeed a literature of the oppressed.[62]

Apocalyptic as a genre flourished in Judaism between 200 BCE and 150 CE approximately, and comes into biblical prominence around the time of the Maccabean revolt. In the Old Testament, the book of Daniel (written around 164 BCE) is its main representative. Scholars are agreed that to make sense of it, we need to appreciate its context:

> The apocalyptic books . . . cannot be understood apart from the religious, political and economic circumstances of the times, nor can the times themselves be understood apart from these books whose hopes and fears echo and re-echo the faith of God's chosen people.[63]

At first sight it presents a bizarre mixture of apparent predictions, grotesque symbols and codes, and sometimes gruesome descriptions.

Jewish apocalyptic literature had its birth among those who felt that this was a significant moment in history and that a stand had to be made. This was, in the beginning, a protest against the Greek occupiers of Judah who were imposing an alien culture. The Judeans saw this as a moral crusade: God was on their side. This was essentially a battle between the forces of good and the forces of evil. You had to know which side you were on; you could trust no-one. There was much demonization. Secret codes were employed among the strategists. Apocalyptic itself was part of the propaganda. At the same time, these were events that made for social cohesion. There was much rhetoric. Apocalyptic was a literary art form that thrived in these times.

The word comes from the Greek for "to reveal", and that is the theological basis of the writings: they purport to reveal God's plan for history. The theological roots of apocalyptic are in the post-exilic embrace of monotheism. If there is only one God, then God must be the creator of all things, and that must include God's design for history. Just as the physical world was ordered, so also God must have designed and ordered time too. So apocalyptic commonly divides the whole of world history up into ages, often describing the events that are planned to take place as one age gives way to another. These are frequently turbulent events, sometimes described as birth-pangs. They involve the conquering of evil so that it might have no place in the new age. This old era is going to end badly, but there will be a new heaven and a new earth, a new city and a new Jerusalem. This, then, is a way of explaining traumatic events, such as those described in Lamentations, as being part of God's plan: not because the people have been found guilty, but rather because God needs to root out the very evil that oppresses them, and the good people are collateral damage.

This literature appealed to its audience because it said that all the things which caused suffering in this age would be overcome in the next. There was no need to feel vulnerable and at the mercy of malign forces, because God the creator of history was truly in control and this was all part of God's plan. The new age would soon be here, and God would wipe every tear from their eyes. We can perhaps understand how this might appeal to Old Testament people, living under occupying regimes, but why was it needed in New Testament times? The answer is that it spoke then to a situation we can still recognize today: a situation in which faith is at odds with experience. In New Testament times, people had been told that Jesus had won a great victory over evil, represented in the book of Revelation by the Roman state, given the cypher "Babylon", reviving memories of exile. But Babylon could have been many places, many systems, many scourges throughout history which, through the eyes of faith, seemed to be stronger than the faith being opposed, which was supposed to have delivered victory.

The book of Revelation affirms faith, urging the faithful to endure and to resist backsliding. In particular, the two temptations of idolatry and immorality are to be rejected. This fight of good against evil is a cosmic battle whose effects are replicated on earth. The great drama has its artistic chorus in eucharistic worship. It presents an enticing vision of a great new future in which the ancient promises of Isaiah that the lion will lie down with the lamb are fulfilled, and all nations will come together in a great celebratory feast in a new Jerusalem, in the shadow of the tree of life, whose leaves are for the healing of the nations. This revives memories of both the wisdom and prophetic traditions of Israel, recapitulating their images and metaphors. It gives people something to rally behind and provides hope and confidence. Importantly, it also promises them vindication: if they endure and persist, they will be vindicated by God. An Old Testament apocalyptic verse that describes the Son of Man bringing the faithful to "the Ancient of Days" on the clouds of heaven, for their vindication (Daniel 7:13), had clear resonance in the New Testament (Mark 14:62; Acts 7:56). It was a text that may have given Jesus an identity as the Son of Man, and helped to develop the idea of "*Parousia*".

This is a very different response to lament from that which could be said to see the church as a foretaste of the Kingdom of God, as proclaimed in the Gospels more generally: a new kind of community, with its gentler and more accessible message that God was no longer to be thought of as fighting wars on behalf of his people, but rather in the weakness of the cross—a God who had emptied himself. Not God the conquering hero, but God the crucified. The apocalyptic vision is exciting and dramatic but has high odds. Two thousand years later, faith is still challenged by experience. We still ask questions in faithful incomprehension and only rarely find ourselves in a religious revolutionary mode; history itself has warned us off that.

To try and give some reality to what looks like a written version of some Xbox fantasy game, and to explain why the economic and political background is important, when teaching students about apocalyptic I have normally resorted to my experience of being a vicar in a south Wales mining village during the Miners' Strike of 1984. The area was not rich but had a definite culture which it felt was under threat from mine closures. Notably, the body set up to resist the closures was called the Coalfields Communities Group, with the stress on community. Although, to the outside world, the miners may have appeared strong, that was in fact a front; they felt vulnerable and weak in the face of the threat posed by the powerful political forces represented by the Government and the Coal Board. There was a sense that we were on the cusp of a great change—this was a moment in history where, no matter what, important things had to be fought for.

As in any war, everyone had to declare which side they were on. Everything was black and white: there was no room for nuance. It was a moral war as perceived by the miners. Mrs Thatcher was not just of a different political or economic opinion; she was the epitome of evil who would stop at nothing to achieve her ends. Sometimes the miners felt they had little in common with their own supposed champion, a union leader called Arthur Scargill. It seemed sometimes, indeed, as if they were just collateral damage in an ideological war over which they had no real control. There was propaganda; the other side was demonized. A folk culture set the whole thing to music, painted heroic pictures, and assumed that God was on the miners' side. Certainly the church in my village was, and it contributed to food kitchens and in other ways, though its main support was moral. I like to think that it provided a place to lament. Apocalyptic writing is shot through with liturgical references. Many of the miners were members of church families; they were good people vilified by the media. I knew flying pickets whose phones were bugged, so they had to communicate in secret code in order not to alert the police to their next target. The following day they would be participating in some church activity. There was real suffering and hardship as the money ran out. Blacklegs, such as there were, had to move away afterwards because memories are long. There was much lament, much bitterness, little forgiveness. In the end the miners lost. The communities lost their culture, the chapels are closing, and in the words of Welsh folk singer Max Boyce, "the pithead baths is a supermarket now".

Personal reflection

The gospel, the good news, is not just for the guilty. It is for the broken. What I ought to have said to my girl in Iraq is not what I did say. On reflection, what she most wanted to be assured about was something that, at that time, I had not taken on board. Her life was one in which you could trust no-one, living in a failed state, where new sectarian identities divided people violently, where human congregation was dangerous and often impossible, where emigration and war casualties had completely undermined family solidarity. The good news that she needed to hear was—and is—that *God-willed human society is possible.* And of course, good news needs some evidence, otherwise it can simply trap good people in a bitter cycle of denial. And the evidence for her was the existence of St George's Church. In the midst of all that is wrong, life-denying and degrading, week by week there is a community that lives from the Eucharist in a different scheme altogether, showing in a small way that it can be done.

Her question raises this question for me: what good news did I want to hear during these past few years? It did not concern forgiveness as a main priority, neither had I any hope of hearing good news about a "cure". Things had gone too far for that. I suppose the good news for me was an affirmation of a worldview I had been commending to others. That was (and is) a worldview that affirms life itself, affirms community, affirms love and service and sacrifice as part of complete, mature, Christ-inspired humanity. My ministry as a preacher had often referred to these things but now I knew them to be true in a new way. I was almost obsessed with getting every last drop of life I could for Sue, and it was good news if by some small gesture, some small achievement, I could feel that for one day at least we had succeeded. I took every opportunity to do "normal" things. We went to the cinema once a week for as long as we could. The last film we saw was the fiftieth-anniversary version of *Grease*. The last full sentence I recall hearing her utter was, "I really enjoyed that." We ate out for as long as that was possible, eventually going to McDonald's once a week because it didn't matter how much mess you made there, and the clientele were particularly non-judgemental. The church community was great at accepting her as she was, and I dressed her as she would have wanted to dress each Sunday morning. I took her to a proper hairdresser's, so she could feel good, and insisted—ignoring the opinions of some carers—that she would not wear a nappy, but would wear the kind of underwear that would make her feel like a woman.

I shall have more to say about atonement and redemption later. Most of the theories about atonement are of their time, and I have to confess they do not speak to me. I think it much more useful to bring to mind situations in which I have seen redemption happen, and then to think about how it happened. They might have been situations of reconciliation, overcoming aggression, or scenarios of apparent hopelessness, often overwhelming in their tragic complexity: the kinds of things to lament about. But if they have been redeemed, it has been through things like forgiveness, loving action, sacrifice on someone's part, or humility. These were exemplified to their ultimate degree by the activity of Christ on the cross, and those who take up a cross and follow him must, I believe, commit themselves to that vocation. This strikes me as a crucially important insight into the human condition. In John's Gospel, there is what appears to be a late addition that we call Chapter 21. It begins in a missional way: Peter is trying to catch fish. But the story moves quickly to the pastoral, as Jesus asks him if he really has grasped what being a follower means: loving Jesus and loving "his sheep". And then, immediately following, there is an account of how it will all end badly, as Jesus indicates "the manner of death by which Peter was to glorify God" (John 21:19 REB). That is the dynamic of discipleship.

Redemption is one of God's surprises and a very special gift to humankind. Carers often admit that they have been changed for the better through their caring experience, and that has been my experience too. What surprised me, though perhaps it shouldn't have, because I have been affected often by seeing care in action, is the effect our relationship had on others. One experience stands out. Our Diocese holds a week-long annual residential Synod, and on one occasion it was decided to provide every participant with a prayer partner. The fact that I was not in charge of the distribution and choice of these partners is demonstrated by the fact that mine was the principal speaker at the event, a revered, retired British bishop whom I knew only by repute. He suggested, after a couple of days, that we might give substance to the idea by a long walk along the beach, taking that opportunity to tell me that he had been moved by observing us together. What brought good news and affirmation to me, hopefully brought it to others. And his telling me that was a hugely pastoral gesture on his part that I have not forgotten.

That awareness of redemption can be very fulfilling. Small things can take on huge significance: she smiled today; she spoke a few words today. And that is not to mention the fun that can break through. As I write that, I have a picture in my mind of Sue treating Veronika and me to a rendition of "Abide with me" on air guitar to a backing track from a CD, having fun.

A footnote to the Miners' Strike: at the end of it all, I was proud to be presented (on behalf of the church) with a National Union of Mineworkers tie as a token of thanks for the support the church was perceived to have given. It's not exactly the crown of life, but I'll settle for it.

The New Testament journey

This is what we have seen so far:

- Originally, lament presupposed a naive view of God's strength, but that was a view projected into the space left by God's silence. In the New Testament, we hear God speak through Jesus.
- That speech concerns two important themes for lamenters. One is the power of God displayed in forgiveness. The other is the power of God displayed in redemption.
- Alongside these, and partly as an alternative response to contemporary faithful incomprehension in the face of experienced oppression, there is the tradition of apocalyptic. This creates a

temporary solution in terms of making sense of suffering, but it also creates an expectation which has not yet been fulfilled.

Suggestions for reflection

- Take yourself back to that situation in Baghdad. What kind of thing might you have said? If you were to make a list of the different kinds of good news which the New Testament contains, would it look like the one on page 74?
- What is the difference between forgiving someone who might have wronged us and forgiveness on a much larger scale? For example, after the Second World War whole nations had to be forgiven, and many individuals found that difficult. Is there a forgiveness too great for us to utter as humans?
- What do you think is the force of a nation making apology for past historical events, such as slavery, in the hope of wiping the slate clean?
- Do you agree that the Church is charged to be a forgiving community? Do you find it so?
- Try to picture yourself as a striking miner in the situation described. What might you have looked for in the Church?

CHAPTER 6

Newport Gwent

Experience

A night at the hospital
When I was first ordained, I served as a curate in Newport Gwent. The parish contained a large regional hospital, where my vicar was the chaplain. As I became a priest, I helped out at the hospital, and especially when he was away on holiday; the summer of 1976 was one such time. There was a long drought, and in south Wales grass fires were common. One evening I was called in by the hospital to see the parents of a small child who was dangerously ill. The family lived in a remote spot in the Valleys, and the child—their only child—had become ill earlier in the day. The father was out fighting fires. They had no phone (no mobiles in those days), and he had the car, so his wife felt she had no option but to wait for him to return, which was some hours later. By this time the child's condition had deteriorated to her present condition.

I was met by the Irish sister of the ward, who had called me. She was a formidable presence and had firm ideas about where my duty lay: I was to baptize the child. Did I want to speak to the parents first? Naturally. We had a long conversation; they were not churchgoers, though they had residual belief. The outcome was that they came to a decision not to baptize the child unless and until she got better. They said they did not want to baptize her as an act of desperation, to make God recognize her in a way that might not otherwise be the case, or to try to bargain with God. If she got better, however, they would baptize her as an act of thanksgiving and acknowledgement of God's love. Later that evening the child died.

I have to say that their decision did not please the sister. Her professionalism prevented her from accusing the parents of consigning

91

the child to hell, so she took it out on me instead, effectively accusing me of a dereliction of duty. But I also have to say that I admired their decision. It said to me that this family was not prepared to embrace a transactional view of religion, in which God might react positively to their performing a particular ritual, in a way that God might not have done otherwise. Any cleric will tell you that, for all our preaching, there still remains plenty of evidence of such attitudes to religion in our churches and in society. It is the view put into the mouth of Satan in Job, and it is the basis of the so-called prosperity gospel. But at its heart is something we can all recognize and perhaps sympathize with: we want what we do to make a difference. We want our prayers and rituals, our behaviour and our actions to be, at least, noticed and, in some cases, reflected in eternal rewards.

Lament is originally open to a transactional interpretation. Such appeals to God need not always be selfish. A famous prayer from an anonymous Jewish inmate, found at the Ravensbrück concentration camp after the war, displays—with the same basic understanding about human agency—commendable generosity.

> Lord, remember not only the people of goodwill, but also those of ill will. But do not remember all the suffering they have inflicted upon us. Remember rather the fruits we have brought, thanks to this suffering: our comradeship, our loyalty, our humility, the courage, the generosity, the greatness of heart that has grown out of this. And when they come to judgment, let all the fruits we have borne be their forgiveness.

A Christian alternative to a transactional view is summed up in two verses of a hymn attributed to St Francis Xavier and translated by Edward Caswall:

> My God, I love thee; not because
> I hope for heaven thereby,
> nor yet because who love thee not
> are lost eternally.

> Thou, O Lord Jesus, thou didst me
> upon the cross embrace;
> for me didst bear the nails and spear,
> and manifold disgrace.

Perhaps the most negative expression of a transactional understanding is found in the kind of lament which complains that we have done everything necessary, and yet misfortune has still befallen us. We want to confront God with the injustice of this. We want to confront God with our catalogue of good works, our attendance register, our accounts that display generous giving, our faithfulness in relationships. We expected better of God. Lament can be our protest at what we see as an absurdity. As Westermann puts it, "It is a protest directed at God to be sure, but it is nevertheless a protest; it does not endure absurdity submissively and patiently: it protests!"[64]

These examples raise a number of questions, with which this chapter will deal from the perspective of New Testament writings:

- How does a Christian, non-transactional understanding of the relationship between God and humankind, based on God's initiative rather than human agency with its consequences for a Christian view of salvation, impact on lament?
- What are the implications of a new revelation of God for the new community of faith, particularly in relation to lament? And does lament have a liturgical place?
- Has lament been rendered redundant by the passion of Jesus, and is endurance now more legitimate for Christians than protest?

Text and commentary

Law and grace
There is an interpretation of "law" in the Old Testament that sees it in transactional terms. In fact, talk of laws and statutes almost *invites* a transactional view, even when it is not intended. That a law-based religion fuels moves towards institutionalism also encourages a transactional

view: keeping the law leads to salvation. This was an interpretation of New Testament Judaism popular at the time of the Reformation; it is easy to see why. Part of the reaction to the Western Church at that time concerned the way in which it was perceived to have institutionalized salvation, to the extent that so-called indulgences (written permits mitigating the effects of sin) could be bought and sold. In the Reformation period there was a great deal of dispute about the *means whereby* an individual is saved. This argument developed into a binary choice between works and grace. Grace was seen as the free and generous gift of God which was offered to those who trusted in God. Works were equated with "the Law" by Reformation writers in a far from subtle way. Their understanding of the Jewish approach to salvation was that it depended on adhering to the law and meeting all its demands. This has influenced, ever since, the work of Protestant scholars who, as well as being suspicious of the sacerdotal context of priestly understandings of church, have tended the see the law in totally negative terms and have taken Paul as their champion, based on that view. There is some evidence for this negative view of law (e.g. Romans 7:4; 8:2-4; Galatians 3:10-14,23-25); Paul is keen, in his letters, to make a distinction between law and grace as a means of salvation. But the post-Reformation Protestant consensus has been challenged by the more nuanced view of E. P. Sanders,[65] who argued that Judaism maintained a view of God's grace: God chose Israel to be his people, but keeping the law does nothing to influence that initiative of God's. Rather, keeping the law maintains membership of the group called Israel, through certain kinds of prescribed behaviour—behaviour which Paul commends (Romans 7:12; 13:8; Galatians 5:13,14). The membership of Israel is no longer ethnically determined (Galatians 6:16).

Paul and salvation
Galatians 1:14 and Philippians 3:4-6 tell us that formerly Paul subscribed to Jewish religious tradition. By his time those "survival mechanisms" of exile discerned by the Priestly writers in the Old Testament—Sabbath, male circumcision and ordered structure—had taken on important religious significance, and along with adherence to the law were part of what would, it was hoped, bring about vindication (or as Paul calls it, justification). This view of religion implies an understanding of God's

power as that of a God "who can if he wants to", but is prevented from doing what he will by the intransigence of the people. It is a view of God's power represented by the disciples James and John, who clearly still believe in a God who can bring down fire from heaven (Luke 9:54, with reference to 2 Kings 1:10,12), as well as by the chief priests and scribes who, at the crucifixion, taunt Jesus: "If you really are the Son of God, save yourself and come down from the cross" (Matthew 27:40 REB). That represents a view that Israel was a people special to God who would one day be "restored" through the agency of a new anointed one, a Messiah in the image of David. But this would only come about through the keeping of the law in all its (by this time) sophisticated detail and complexity. Paul, on the other hand, is fascinated by what the crucifixion says about God and salvation. He believes the cross is the basis of the new religion (1 Corinthians 2:2). What does it mean to believe in a God who can be crucified? What is the significance of the cross? He concludes that not only did Jesus physically die there, but that the whole understanding of Jewish religion died there too. Colossians 2:14 (REB) puts it plainly: "he has cancelled the bond which was outstanding against us with its legal demands; he has set it aside, nailing it to the cross." And although not all scholars agree that Colossians was written by Paul, that sentiment is consistent with his undisputed writings.

This is particularly true in Galatians where he argues the point, in Chapter 4, by reference to an allegory comparing two women, one free and one a slave. Both have sons. "Now this is an allegory: these women are two covenants. One woman, in fact, is Hagar, from Mount Sinai, bearing children for slavery. Now Hagar is Mount Sinai in Arabia and corresponds to the present Jerusalem, for she is in slavery with her children. But the other woman corresponds to the Jerusalem above; she is free, and she is our mother." (Galatians 4:24–26). He says directly, " . . . Listen! I, Paul, am telling you that if you let yourselves be circumcised, Christ will be of no benefit to you. Once again I testify to every man who lets himself be circumcised that he is obliged to obey the entire law. You who want to be justified by the law have cut yourselves off from Christ; you have fallen away from grace. For in Christ Jesus neither circumcision nor uncircumcision counts for anything; the only thing that counts is faith working through love." (Galatians 5:2–4,6).

In fact, Paul's view of grace is not dissimilar to the Old Testament Covenant idea of *hesed*. And just as *hesed* describes God's nature but also suggests an attitude for covenanters to hold and to translate into positive action, so grace has the same function, not now in response to election as a special ethnic people of God, but in response to God's act in Jesus for all humankind. The promises of God are now open to all. The choice is not so much between law and grace as between national entitlement and exclusiveness, on the one hand, and God's generous universality on the other. It remains the case still that the idea of covenant is central to mending broken relationships. Whether we accept this interpretation or not, we are presented through Paul's letters with a vibrant and dynamic view of God: not as one who demands adherence to a law, but rather one who is characterized by giving and granting (Romans 5:5; 12:3,6; 15:15; 1 Corinthians 1:4; 3:5,10; 12:7,8, etc.).

Grace
The law was itself regarded as a gift in its time, and especially by the authors of Deuteronomy, but now we have evidence of the supreme act of divine giving which Paul calls "grace" (in Greek "*charis*", which gives us the English word "charity"). Grace translates a Hebrew word meaning "to stoop". Graceful action is that of the strong towards the weak, the greater toward the lesser. Such giving has to be intentional because it is boundary-crossing and, if you like, both unnatural and unnecessary. There is no *need*, on the face of it, for the rich to give to the poor or for the strong to protect the weak or for the secure to shield the vulnerable. Indeed, the teaching of Greek philosophy would consider unnatural boundary-crossing activity as quite dangerous.[66] It is this reckless act of God, prompted by his love, which excites Paul's imagination. And so the character of Christian religion is thanksgiving as a response to that love, but for Paul that is not a passive thing. Thanksgiving is dynamic, placing responsibilities on us to imitate God and be graceful to others in our turn, and so to construct communities of thanksgiving (the Greek word is the one that gives us "eucharist"), which will be communities of graceful response.

There is much scholarly debate about all aspects of Paul's theology, which has been abbreviated here. Particularly important for the view taken above is the question of whether "the faith *of* Christ" uses a subjective or objective genitive—that is, does it refer to our faith in God or God's faith in us?[67] The key texts are Romans 3:22; Galatians 2:16,20; 3:22 and Philippians 3:9. I take it as subjective, that is, Christ affirms us. Whatever Judaism believed, this startling reversal of what "religious" people think of God has a profound effect on what we think we are doing through lament. What cannot be denied is that the graceful act of God in Christ is central to Paul's understanding of God's nature, and that our relationship with Christ—and/or his with us—offers an alternative view of the goals of religion to that of Paul's former Judaism. It is important to have that context in mind as we look at some specific passages relating to our theme: these come from 2 Corinthians where Paul considers the power of God.

Power and weakness

2 Corinthians "seems to envisage the restoration of a fractured relationship between the Corinthians and Paul", says Ian Boxall in a guide to the New Testament.[68] At 3:6, Paul writes of the power of God which "empowers us as ministers of a new covenant, not written but spiritual". He picks up the theme of ministry in Chapter 4 (from verse 1), and argues in Chapter 5 that God's initiative in Christ is the model for a "ministry of reconciliation", in which ministers are "ambassadors for Christ" (5:18,20).

The opening verses of 2 Corinthians echo the opening verses of Deutero-Isaiah (Isaiah 40:1; cf. 51:3), which are directed towards people who are suffering in exile and need consolation. 2 Corinthians 1:3-8 contains ten occurrences of the word "comfort" (Greek "*parakaleo*", the word group which gives the name "paraclete" or "comforter" to the Holy Spirit in John's Gospel e.g. John 14:16; 15:26; 16:7). This is not, as in Isaiah, a straightforward message of good news. In the first place, it is linked to Christ's sufferings: we may take comfort in sharing in his sufferings (1:7). Secondly, the word used for the suffering of Christians is the Greek word "*thlipsis*" (1:4,6), which is used of very severe trials of the kind that might require consolation. It is sometimes used to describe the sufferings at the end of the age (Matthew 24:21; Revelation 7:14)—but, importantly, the point of receiving this comfort is not personal reassurance. It is rather that, having been given this comfort from a God who has also suffered, we may then comfort others who need to be comforted in their own "*thlipsis*". "For the Christian, the comfort and strength God gives isn't intended to be an end in itself; it issues in further comfort as the comforted become comforters. God's grace in afflictions has a *transforming* effect; it touches lives in need with the result that they touch others."[69] Part of being a community of graceful response is being a comforting community, and a community intimately connected with Christ himself, through sharing sufferings.

We see Paul's understanding of the power of God later in 2 Corinthians, in what many commentators think is a separate letter but one also written by Paul. In Chapter 11, Paul recites an impressive CV, but this is not something he wants to trumpet. He is what he is by the grace of God (1 Corinthians 15:10). He has learned, from his own experience of suffering, something of the nature of God. We read in 2 Corinthians 12:7 that Paul has made supplication to God—a mini-lament—on account of what he calls "a thorn in the flesh". The response he gets is, "My grace is all you need; power is most fully seen in weakness" (12:9 REB). Having received this word, Paul continues: "I am therefore happy to boast of my weaknesses, because then the power of Christ will rest upon me." That is, if you like, the response to his lament.

We saw how, in the Old Testament, the faithful wanted God to intervene in a demonstration of power. They did not want to have to regard him as a defeated God. In the New Testament, a different picture is emerging, one that is specifically Christian. In Acts 2:1–21, we have a definitive example of God's power, personified in the Holy Spirit. This is the fulfilment of the promise Jesus made after the resurrection (Luke 24:48,49), that the disciples would be filled with power and that they would be witnesses. As the subsequent story of the church in Acts continues, we see that the power given is the power to speak and to bear witness: to witness to the power of love and forgiveness. The power of God will be expressed in the Spirit and through the witnesses who make up the nascent Church. It is an enabling power.

There is a further important component to Paul's theology relevant to our theme: his innovative description of the Church as the body of Christ is a multi-faceted theological image. In 1 Corinthians 10–15 we see the variety of its applications. It can refer to the eucharist (10:17; 11:24,27,29);

thus it can refer to Christ's broken body and (in Chapter 15) to his risen body. It can be a description of the diversity of membership and ministry in the church (12:14–31; Romans 12:1; Ephesians 1:23). For Paul, it also enables a very personal sense of identity with Christ's sufferings, most notably at Philippians 3:10 and (perhaps) 2:17. In Colossians 1:24 he says, "I am now rejoicing in my sufferings for your sake, and in my flesh I am completing what is lacking in Christ's afflictions for the sake of his body, that is, the church." This is a remarkable claim—the sufferings of Christians are, in fact, to be understood as Christ's continuing sufferings.

In summary: in the Old Testament, lamenting people, suffering and oppressed people, longed for a God perceived as powerful to speak, act, demonstrate God's power and save or deliver. In the New Testament Epistles of Paul, we see something new emerging:

- God in Jesus is a suffering God, a crucified God;
- the Church as the Body of Christ continues his sufferings in the world;
- being connected to Christ in his sufferings is itself a form of comfort;
- there is a power in such apparent weakness: the power to forgive, love and care. It is the power of grace.

And from Acts and John:

- The Church witnesses to this God and is enabled to do so by the power of God personified in the Holy Spirit, the Comforter.

So what does this tell us about the Church and lament? Certainly that the Church is called to be a body responsive to lament, as a comforting, witnessing, loving and forgiving community.

Lament or endurance?
The eclipse of lament *per se* in the New Testament is not due simply to the triumph of sin over suffering as a controlling universal motif in a theology of salvation. It has also to do with the legitimacy of lament as opposed to, or compared with, silent endurance. This question is related both to our

understanding of God's nature, and particularly the power of God, and to the graceful personhood of Jesus. It will have implications for the Church as a body which continues Christ's sufferings in the world. Apart from the Gospels, the New Testament book containing most references to suffering in proportion to its length is 1 Peter. The term *"pascho"* for "suffering" is one word that connects Christ's sufferings to those of believers. The word has no exact Hebrew equivalent, since *"pascho"* implies a certain passivity foreign to the Old Testament context. It is used forty-two times in the New Testament, normally (though not exclusively) in connection with Christ's sufferings, and that is how it is used in 1 Peter. The reference is always initially to Christ's death, and the usage stresses that this forms a model for the behaviour of Christians (1 Peter 2:21–23; 3:18; 4:1). This is despite the fact that Jesus is not presented by the Gospel writers as using *pascho* in descriptions of the future sufferings of his followers. Yet 1 Peter's use of the word stresses the identity, rather than mere similarity, between Christ's sufferings and those of believers (2:19; 3:14,17; 4:1,15,19; 5:10). The suffering of believers is described in detail: 2:19 refers to receiving unjust punishment from overbearing masters; 4:15 describes another practical situation in which Christians may appear before the courts; 3:14 describes "suffering for doing right"; 5:9 relates local sufferings (cognate noun) to those of the "brotherhood" throughout the world. These examples are always of suffering inflicted by the powerful on the disadvantaged, and they are all capable of being understood as the sufferings of Christ. The noun used for Christ's sufferings at 1:11, 4:13 and 5:1 is pathemata. The same noun occurs in 2 Corinthians 1:5. Here again we see the identity between the believers' suffering and those of Christ.

Although there has been debate about the severity of suffering described in 1 Peter, the consensus of scholarly opinion is that relatively local harassment and persecution—rather than anything bigger and state-sanctioned—are in view. The Greek word that usually describes them is *"peirasmos"*, which refers in most settings to a kind of moral testing. Other terms of interest include the verb to grieve, *"lupeo"* (1 Peter 1:6; 2:19), while *"loidoreo"* (to abuse or insult) is a less common word, used to describe events at Jesus' trial. His response supplies a model for Christians to follow (2:21,23). The verb *"oneidizo"*, describing verbal abuse, is also part of the Passion vocabulary (Matthew 27:44; Mark

15:32). Two other words are of note: "*ekdikesis*" (1 Peter 2:14), meaning punishment, though not the normal Greek word for this, and "*kolaphizo*" which Peter uses of what might be expected from masters (2:20), but also describes the blows Jesus suffered at his trial (Matthew 26:67; Mark 14:65). These are all powerful terms in connecting physical, everyday suffering of Christians to the severe sufferings of Christ.

In the face of these real sufferings—about which, in other circumstances, people may have lamented—Christians are told to endure just as Christ did. This suffering is a kind of refining (1 Peter 1:7; 4:12). Christians are to submit themselves to authority without protest, no matter how unjustly they are treated (2:12-19). "If you endure when you are beaten for doing wrong, where is the credit in that? But if you endure when you do right and suffer for it, you have God's approval. For to this you have been called, because Christ also suffered for you, leaving you an example, so that you should follow in his steps." (2:20,21). In the same vein, "But even if you do suffer for doing what is right, you are blessed." (3:14). This kind of sentiment is not restricted to 1 Peter. The Epistle of James, which is addressed to the "dispersion of the twelve tribes" (with echoes of the "*paroikoi*" of 1 Peter 1:1), makes the message of endurance its first priority. In the face of trials ("*peirasmoi*"), "and let endurance have its full effect, so that you may be mature and complete, lacking in nothing". (James 1:4). The usual New Testament word for endurance is "*hypomone*", occurring more than twenty times. Ironically, the Epistle of James uses it (5:11) to describe what is often translated as "the patience of Job", when demonstrably—although he "endures"—Job does not do so without lament. James urges his hearers to be patient ("*makrothumeo*") no fewer than five times in five verses (James 5:7-11; cf. the use of the word to describe patience as an attribute of God, 1 Peter 3:20).

Given those examples it is not difficult to see how lament declined. On the one hand, salvation has come to mean saving bad people from sin rather than good people from distress and suffering. And on the other, suffering patiently and silently has come to take a central place in Christian discipleship, both as a means of commitment to Christ, honouring his suffering, and as a means of self-discipline and witness. Moreover, the Church itself has come to be described as, characteristically, a community of those who continue Christ's sufferings. It is interesting to see whether lament has any residual traces in this understanding of church.

The replacement of lament by endurance has its own problems. First, it can encourage denial about suffering, which may lead to an acceptance of the sufferings of others. Sölle says, "Only those who themselves are suffering will work for the abolition of conditions under which people are exposed to senseless, patently unnecessary suffering, such as hunger, oppression, or torture."[70] Second, it can encourage a kind of Christian masochism which is completely self-centred, and third, that can in turn lead to the glorification of martyrdom, in which Jesus himself is seen primarily as a martyr.

The Church as household

If we take 1 Peter as an example, how do we imagine what church represents for its members, in terms of maintaining Christ's sufferings? This is presented as a letter to scattered exiles (1:1; 2:11). The Greek word that describes these people is "*paroikoi*" (from which we get the English word "parish"). According to an important publication by John Elliott in 1981, this is an identifiable social group within the regions and ancient kingdoms of what is now western Turkey.[71] They were technically "resident aliens": that is, they were foreigners, the kind of people who might nowadays have temporary residence and work permits but few civil rights. As foreigners they were suspect. As Christians, they were also an easy target for scapegoating when anything went wrong. Natural disasters could be blamed on their disdain for the civic gods; they could be accused of upsetting social cohesion; the Jews didn't want to be associated with them, for fear of being confused with them and losing some concessions they had received from the state, such as the right to keep the Sabbath and organize synagogues. That is the context of their "trials of many kinds" (1:6).

The picture that 1 Peter draws to describe the Christian community in these circumstances is that of the *household*. Members are living stones (2:5) to be built into a spiritual house (rather than a "spiritual temple" as in the *Revised English Bible*, for example). The long section from 2:11 to 3:12 sets out rules for living in such a household, and 4:17 sees the Church described as "God's own household". The Greek word for house is "*oikos*".

Elliot's thesis is that Peter's message is of an *oikos* for the *paroikoi*—that is, a home for the homeless. As in the many other pictures of the Church in the New Testament, it is an image which connects the faithful with Christ himself. That is true both in the physical illustration—they are the living stones, he is the head cornerstone (2:4)—and in the social illustration— they are members of the family, he is the head of the household. This is a view of church that retains the Covenant aspirations of holiness (2:5) whilst completely redefining the concept of institutional hierarchy. Interpersonal relations, as in a family, are most important here. Even the one designation that sounds like an "office" in the church is not just a presbyter, but a fellow (Greek "*sym*") presbyter (5:1).

From the internal evidence, we might imagine that the church community offers a consolatory setting for sharing each other's sufferings, and that "scriptures" such as the letter addressed to them offer material for reflection on their experience. Theologically, the thrust of the epistle is closer to an apocalyptic understanding than any other. The sufferings mentioned at 1:6 are preceded by the promise of "the hope of an inheritance reserved in heaven" (1:4 REB), guaranteed by the power ("*dunamis*") of God (1:5). The lowly situation of the addressees is turned on its head by the claim that it gives them a unique opportunity to witness by an alternative lifestyle to that of "Gentiles" (2:12).

One final question we might ask is, "Did the Early Church get it right?" Westermann thinks it did not. He is not convinced that endurance should represent the new normal. "There is no passage in the Gospels that suggests that Jesus saw his task to be one of convincing the sufferer that one must bear suffering patiently."[72] He believes that insufficient notice has been taken of the intentions of the Evangelists, in the use of Psalm 22 in their accounts of the passion. "If the gospel story of the passion is presented in the words of Psalm 22, the authors quite obviously wanted to say that Christ had taken up the lament of those people who suffer, that he too had entered into suffering."[73] If he is correct, then God—the one who has hitherto been the object of lament—becomes its subject.

Westermann's regrets are echoed by Brueggemann in a recent contribution to a collection of essays on the theme of theology and mental health.[74] Commenting on the psalms of lament, he writes: "How odd it is that these rich resources of the community of faith . . . have been almost completely lost in the life of the Church, being absent (except for Psalm 22) in the liturgical sequence of the Church."[75] He believes that this absence derives from a cultural avoidance of honesty and truth-telling, and is further evidence of a society in denial. He believes that truth-telling has become a private and largely secularized practice (through pastoral care and counselling). The reduction by the Church of the variety of human emotional responses to the single one of guilt is also responsible, and Brueggemann cites the conclusion of Fredrik Lindström: "The confession of sin is not an element in the classical individual complaint Psalms, and the motif of sin, in the few cases in which it occurs, hardly functions as indication of the reason for the affliction."[76] Whilst this is a point well made, the basic theme here is surely the one to do with the theology of salvation. Political salvation has a definite "result", and once that result is achieved, salvation no longer has force. A more universal understanding of that from which we need to be saved has to be found, and sin is a less risky choice than suffering.

Journeying on

Two main alternative tracks are becoming apparent:

1. The apocalyptic track, in which enduring present suffering is seen as a test of discipleship, pending vindication through some future intervention by God. The suffering is a necessary condition of transition to the next age. All present suffering is part of God's plan, and he is in control of events which ultimately will lead to a good outcome. Waiting patiently is what Christians should do. Lament is not articulated. Utterances of those who have suffered, now redeemed, are represented as songs of praise, shorn of complaint or supplication (Revelation 4:11; 5:13; 7:12; 11:16; 15:3; 19:3,4). This track is not confined to Revelation, being also evidenced, for example, in 1 Peter.[77]
2. The Pauline track as outlined above, in which God who empties himself and is crucified lives on in the life of the Church and

shares its sufferings, as they in turn share God's sufferings as seen in the sufferings of the world.

Both of these tracks find expression in the Eucharist. Songs of praise meet with prayers of honest truthful offering, memories of Christ's lament, and hopes of redemption. Both tracks see this as a new statement of the Covenant, representing a fresh beginning and a new normal (Matthew 26:28; Mark 14:24; 1 Corinthians 11:25; Revelation 21:7).

Personal reflection

The modern Greek words for family and home do not appear in the New Testament, where the word *"oikos"* can describe them both with a wide range of possible translations, one of which is "household". The strength of that word became apparent to me during my journey with Sue. In the early years, the desire to maintain her dignity and our privacy had meant that our house, once a social hub and place of entertaining, meeting and gathering, had become a solitary kind of place, a shadow of its former self with a much-denuded sense of life. It was a fortress.

There came a point where that privacy could be maintained no longer. As is often the case for fathers, the catalyst was the insistent voice of our daughter. She and her family came to stay with us every year, and we saw a lot of them when we were in the UK (ironically, Sue spent three months there not long after we moved, to look after our three grandchildren in that family while our daughter recovered from a debilitating illness). On one of their summer visits, our daughter told me I had to get help. She said that with everything else that now needed to be done for her mother, I should at least have someone else to do the cleaning. Sue was reluctant and thought we could cope "until she got better", but eventually I persuaded her to accept help, and we advertised. I discounted the first people I saw, on the grounds that they clearly regarded Sue as an invalid and not a person of worth; but then, following a recommendation from parishioners, we found someone who turned out to be really excellent. Veronika had been a nanny but had now started her own cleaning business. From the start, she and Sue connected, and as time went on she became much more than a cleaner, rather more of a household steward and friend. She came everywhere with us, including to the UK on a couple of occasions, and was a real companion to Sue. But that involved "letting someone else in" to what had been a very intense personal setting. Before, we had been a couple. Now, we were a household.

As time went on and Sue deteriorated to the point where she needed specialist nursing care—two agencies refused to come any more, saying they felt they could not guarantee the safety of their staff—the household increased. There was a pool of nurses, as well as an occupational therapist (Nikki), who were in and out of the house as I had need. Somehow, the caring atmosphere bred quite a close sense of community. Perhaps it was that I was a priest, but confidences were shared and the visitors' family difficulties often rehearsed. I came to know their stories, while becoming resigned—at the same time—to my house being full of strangers from whom no secrets were hid concerning what I would once have called our "private life". But the house, in a sense, came to life again. I began to understand the positive side of what a "household" felt like.

I had always thought the designation of the Church as "the family of God" rather twee. It summoned up in my mind something quite insular, naive and indulgent, but that perception changed as well. In Cyprus, we too were foreigners, resident aliens (though certainly not shunned—I have a deep affection for Cyprus and its people), and the church became for me a focus of belonging in a way I hadn't quite recognized before. Perhaps unwittingly, I found myself preaching more about our vocation of welcome, and of sharing suffering. I think the character of the church changed a little. Perhaps it had always been like that. Perhaps my experience was like that of Yevgeny Yevtushenko (1933–2017) in these lines from his famous poem "Zima Junction":

> If the way I see you now is not the way
> In which we saw you once, if in you
> What I see now is new
> It was by self-discovery I found it.

Certainly St Helena's Church was a lifeline for me, and in the end it was the last place I could go to with Sue in a social setting, the one in which she was treated as (and could feel like) a fellow human being. That was thanks to the heroic efforts of those who sat with her during services and tolerated her idiosyncrasies—painstakingly marking her hymn book with numbered stickers only for her to pick them all out again before the service started—to whom I shall ever be grateful. Every Sunday I would ask if she had enjoyed herself; every Sunday she would say, "Yes".

My bishop insisted that his archdeacons should wear purple cinctures—the sash that we wore as a kind of belt with a cassock—to signify that we were part of the "bishop's household". That too struck me as odd originally. But again, as I found in him a confidant, and he also had a senior priest to speak to, the concept of household began to make more sense than that of simply "friends" or "colleagues". We had a shorthand way of my telling him how I felt, particularly if it had been a really bad night, or if Sue had been particularly agitated. It was based on a short Robert Frost poem called "Lodged":

> The rain to the wind said,
> "You push and I'll pelt."
> They so smote the garden bed
> That the flowers actually knelt,
> And lay lodged—though not dead.
> I know how the flowers felt.[78]

On several days, in answer to the Bishop's question I would simply say, "I know how the flowers felt".

I know that Christians are not meant to feel comfortable. An influential, autobiographical book by a bishop working in apartheid South Africa takes its title from G. K. Chesterton's 1911 poem, "The Ballad of the White Horse":

> I tell you naught for your comfort,
> Yea, naught for your desire,
> Save that the sky grows darker yet
> And the sea rises higher.

In spite of that, it is great to feel comforted, and to know that others want you to be so. I can certainly see more clearly what it means to be a community that shares Christ's sufferings.

It is easy for worship to continue in complete ignorance of the real world, at some ontological level with angels and archangels rather than refugees and the homeless and the demented, even when they are banging their pots and pans outside.

Suggestions for reflection

- Recalling the story from the hospital at the start of this chapter, where do your sympathies lie? What does that tell you about your view of God?
- Read through 2 Corinthians 1:1–11. How important is "consolation" in the agenda of any faith community you are part of?
- What does the idea of the Church as the "household of faith" suggest to you? How do you think it compares with the "Body of Christ"? Which image do you prefer?

CHAPTER 7

Lancashire

Experience

Marie's story
At the end of August 1959, a six-year-old girl named Marie was sent from her home in Oldham, Lancashire, to an orphanage run by a Catholic order of nuns. She was not an orphan, but her family was growing at such an alarming rate—her mother was pregnant almost continuously—that they no longer had money enough to feed and clothe them all, so she and her brother, as the two eldest, were being "taken into care". Her account of what happened to her there, written sixty years later, has all the hallmarks of a lament. One nun, Sister Isobel, oversaw a regime of bullying and abuse—spiritual, physical and sexual—which was quite terrifying, and its trauma had lasting effects. What made all this worse was the tragic irony that the perpetrators of the abuse were those meant to be caring because of their Christian conviction. What resulted was a cruel caricature of religion. She writes:

> On Ash Wednesday in February 1961, there was a special service in the chapel to mark the start of Lent. Sister Isobel fussed over the priest as though he was the pope himself. "This is the start of Lent," she told us viciously. "Forty days and forty nights of suffering. And it was all for you. You are all sinners, every one of you." I shifted uncomfortably. I had such bad thoughts about Sister Isobel. I noticed she had not included herself in the list of sinners. I noticed that *she* was showing no gratitude and no humility. But I felt uneasy as she preached, I feared that she could read my mind and she was speaking directly to me.

> This God was completely different to the one I'd prayed to back at home. The God my mother knew was the one who fixed broken limbs and heads, sent food when there was none in the cupboard, and let us off when we were naughty. But the God here was a tyrant and a bully, ordering his wife, Sister Isobel (or was she married to the priest?) to beat and torture us and make us cry.[79]

Marie Hargreaves' book takes us through all three stages described by Brueggemann in his *Message of the Psalms*. First there is *orientation* in a loving family, albeit a very poor one, before the dreadful *disorientation* of the Convent at Billinge, where the abuse occurred. In Marie's case, there was thankfully a *reorientation*, which she was able to describe, looking back at the age of 63. After her husband of thirty years died, and following other tragic events and deaths in her life, she "found solace in the church". She writes:

> With [husband] Jack gone, I reached out to the church for help. It was a decision which I knew people might struggle to understand. But as time passed, the church became another family for me, a community. As well as attending mass, I helped out at church, reading the lessons and organizing social events. All my life, I had strived for acceptance and belonging. The church had taken all that away from me when I was small and now it was handing it all back.[80]

She felt strong enough to return to her place of captivity, and subsequently saw a counsellor who was surprised that she did not feel anger and bitterness. Marie came to realize those things were corrosive, and that the only way to be rid of the corrosion was through forgiveness. "Over the past 50 years, I had moved on, albeit subconsciously. I was breathing clean air now. I had forgiven her."[81] This reads like Psalm 30 in modern dress. In fact, her book concludes with Marie having agreed to take up a job as housekeeper for a priest in Ireland.

Alongside the obvious traumas of terrorism, pandemic and warfare experienced over the last quarter of a century, the bringing to public notice of instances of abuse, both private and institutional, often on a huge scale, has also been a reason for some writers to return to the theme of lament. There have been the proven allegations against the film mogul Harvey Weinstein, which gave birth to the #MeToo movement, and those against TV personality Jimmy Savile which prompted the police enquiry into abuse more generally: Operation Yewtree. These latter allegations were all the more shocking because Savile was regarded as a modern-day saint by many people. His life on the surface appeared to epitomize sacrificial service to the vulnerable and disabled; but beneath the surface it emerged that he had abused over five hundred vulnerable people. That same sense of betrayal accompanied the growing chorus of allegations about abuse in children's homes and especially within churches, both institutions publicly committed to the care of people they were actually exploiting.

Others have felt betrayed more recently. The posthumous investigation into the alleged abuse of women by Jean Vanier—founder of the L'Arche Communities and author of a number of books on spirituality and human community which have transformed the lives of many readers—has led to people feeling angry, let down and confused. One consequence of the scandals has been that practical theologians have begun to take a professional interest in the whole field of abuse. In 2005, Stephen Pattison and Gordon Lynch chose abuse as a practical example to illustrate how their discipline worked: "One consequence of taking the contemporary lived experience of abuse survivors seriously is that sharp difficult questions can be raised about the nature of religious belief and practice." Among those questions was, "Does lament or rage have an appropriate role in the life of the survivor?"[82]

Text and commentary

Our fault?
There is something about Sister Isobel's introduction to Lent that will leave all of us uneasy. We recognize her hypocrisy, and yet the Ash Wednesday liturgies do remind us harshly of our sin. The question about whether we deserve the bad things that happen takes us back to the

psalms of lament, and the heart of the question: is suffering or sin the determining narrative in human misfortune? Are we innocent or guilty? Am I somehow responsible for the abuse I am suffering? Did I bring this rape on myself? J. David Pleins examines this question in his book, *The Psalms: Songs of Tragedy, Hope and Justice*.[83] He notes that the Old Testament contains different theological strands. The Deuteronomistic writers (responsible for Joshua to 2 Kings, and with close links to eighth- and seventh-century prophets) clearly believe that Israel has a moral and theological responsibility for her own downfall. "Similarly, the writers of Proverbs blame the poor for their suffering as a punishment for laziness. In contrast, the book of Job counters Israel's standard theology of rewards and punishments by posing the counter argument: What about the innocent who suffer?"[84] He goes on to point out that few of the lament psalms link suffering with transgression, Psalms 38 and 51 being the main exceptions. Psalm 26 makes a robust challenge to this view: "I have led a blameless life, and put unfaltering trust in you. Test me, Lord, and try me, putting my heart and mind to the proof" (Psalm 26:1,2 REB). Other examples include Psalms 13; 23; 24 and 43:2. Pleins wonders whether we harbour deep-down feelings of guilt that obscure our view: "Worship based on the lament moves us beyond guilt feelings to confront a situation that is really out of our hands."[85] Once we have made that movement we are free to confront God: "'Has his steadfast love ceased for ever? Are his promises at an end for all time? Has God forgotten to be gracious? Has he in anger shut up his compassion?' And I say, 'It is my grief that the right hand of the Most High has changed.'" (Psalm 77:8–10).

It is disturbing that abusers can be confused with traditional pictures of God. Hilary Cashman quotes one survivor of child abuse: "I prayed to God to stop the abuse and when he didn't, I felt he must be allowing it. This must be what I was put here for, to be abused."[86] Hints of the questioning in Lamentations are there. Another survivor, as an adult, wondering whether the church might have resources to help her, reports on a day course she attended: "I'm not a Christian, but I was open to the idea that it might have something helpful to offer. We were taken aback by the hymns and prayers at the beginning of the day—talking about God as Father and 'Him' and 'His power'. If you've been on the receiving end of abusive power, you may not want to sing about the power and glory of God."[87]

The faces of God

Kathleen O'Connor is sensitive to this kind of testimony. As we have seen, she believes that robust confrontation of God is part of what Lamentations calls us to. She is not afraid to use the word "abuse", even of God. "The predominant opinion among [the speakers in Lamentations] is that God is cruel and violently abusive. The God who should protect and cherish [Jerusalem] has battered and harassed her in every way short of killing her."[88] In modern testimony, abuse is accompanied by a sense of loneliness and isolation. This is particularly true in domestic abuse of women by men. Phones are checked or taken away. Friends are discouraged. There is no-one to turn to. That is linked with the sense of powerlessness that comes when the ability to make choices is removed. Many survivors speak about how power operated in the relationships with their abusers, and how the abuser made it clear that power resided with them. Often there was a sense of inevitability—that this was something inescapable. The inner thoughts of the abused are revealed. "Is it my fault (cf. Lamentations 1:5)? I'm not sure I believe myself—this can't be happening. Is this just how the world is, and I have to come to terms with it?" Those in whom some people had put ultimate trust had betrayed that trust, with an inevitable sense that meaning in life had been lost or obscured. All of these feelings—isolation, powerlessness, defencelessness, misplaced guilt, confusion and loss of trust—are features to be found in Lamentations. "If God is abusive, victims of abuse are without refuge, tyrants and bullies cannot be restrained, and love can never be trusted."[89]

A modern Jewish perspective is provided by David Blumenthal. His standpoint is that God actually *is* sometimes abusive, and is morally justified in being so. The appropriate mode of address is thus exactly that provided by Lamentations: namely, protest. He gives an example by juxtaposing a reading of Psalm 27 with a commentary by a (Christian) girl of sixteen who has been raped. A couple of verses will give a taste of what we might call unreconstructed lament. Psalm 27:1: "[W]hom then should I fear?" The response is, "[A]nyone. I have no walls, no protection, no structure. I am just standing amidst rubble. What do you mean, 'Whom do I fear?' Everyone." Or again, Psalm 27:4: "I have asked but one thing of the LORD. . . that He conceal me in His *sukka* on the day of evil." Again, the response is combative and robust: "If you say you are my protector, then protect me. If you cannot protect me, then at least tell me so. Don't pretend you can conceal me, protect me or shield me. Don't pretend to be a rock or a shepherd."[90]

O'Connor is one of the few writers prepared to address full-on the references in Lamentations to God as abuser. Whilst institutions are accused of being afraid for their reputations in relation to abuse allegations, it is also the case that many writers, like Job's "comforters", want to put God's reputation beyond scrutiny, and so begin their arguments with a number of givens about God. God is loving and merciful, faithful, patient and liberating. The evidence then has to be fixed around those axioms. This is particularly evidenced in what we might call "the search for green shoots". In the five poems of Lamentations, there are just a couple of verses which we have described as axioms of faith that the faithful cling to persistently, despite the evidence. Some writers refer to them as if they were the main point of the book.[91] We have noted that psalms of lament often have a distinct shift of emotion, from lament towards praise, and we have interpreted that either as a liturgical interjection, to remind the congregation of those axioms of faith, despite the evidence and evident loss of confidence, or as a genuine description , psychologically, of how hope flickers on and off in difficult circumstances.

Robert Davidson is typical in both accepting that Israel deserved what they experienced and asserting God's consistency:

> The darkness of disaster, *though richly deserved* [my italics], cannot be God's final word to the community. They remain his servants, his people, who may confidently expect to experience in the future, as they have done in the past, his steadfast-love and his dependability.[92]

The Evangelical Alliance's Director for Scotland, Fred Drummond, is responsible for an online resource on the theology and practice of lament. His reflection on Psalm 5 notes the author's "frustration" and "discouragement" at seeing bad people prosper (while bad things happen to good people), but continues, "Yet I know there is a higher power, with unfailing love who shields and protects me."[93] This is his main theme in the interpretation.

N.T. Wright's online article "Five Things to Know About Lament" tells us that lament is *"an appeal to God based on confidence in His character"*.[94] Of the five things he says we need to know about God from the evidence of laments, the first three are that laments are hymns of praise, they are a proof of the relationship with God, and they are a pathway to intimacy with God. This is in stark contrast to O'Connor; for her, the author of Lamentations "arrives at hope only after hope has vanished". Finally, "Lamentations has no happy ending; the divine-human relationship is shattered, and God neglects, abuses, and rejects them, perhaps forever. God's abandonment of them ends the book."[95] The question is to what extent the New Testament revelation of God is an antidote to what the writer of Lamentations believes, or to what extent that anger towards God is still, pastorally, to be encouraged.

Witness

From the perspective of the speakers in Lamentations, this is not so much a book about God's unfailing goodness as about the importance of their own witness, and in relation to present-day concerns about abuse, the opportunity for witness has been readily taken. With the new opportunity to speak, new emotions are released. The sense of betrayal is palpable. This often leads to a questioning of everything that the abuser represents, and so people rubbish the formerly revered writings of Vanier, or—unlike Marie Hargreaves—turn their backs on a Church which had formerly given their lives form and meaning. For many, coming to terms with the lying that had gone on has raised new (and sometimes cynical) questions about truth: wondering whether truth is anything more than the narrative of the powerful. It was the people and institutions with reputations who were believed. Above all, there is a rage at institutions like the Church which value their own reputations more than the suffering of the innocent; this is often seen as continuing the abuse by other means. Alongside this, Christian writers and scholars have begun to show more impatience with churches that have forgotten their vocation to be "a serious house on serious earth", as Larkin puts it. They continue in denial of the pain in the world, or perhaps more charitably, they are aware of it but are stunned into silence by it.

It was such an experience of church worship that prompted John Swinton to look seriously at the loss of lament in churches today, precisely at points where there might be said to be a need for a response of lament.[96] His book *Raging with Compassion* is primarily, as its subtitle suggests (*Pastoral Responses to the Problem of Evil*), just that kind of response, and it begins by expressing dissatisfaction with the way in which theodicy— the attempt to systematize an answer to questions about evil—is carried on at an academic, theoretical and philosophical level: "Rarely do the specifics of the lived reality of the human experience of evil, pain, and suffering enter into the philosophical equation."[97] Having given examples of suffering nowadays, Swinton proposes a theodicy that does not begin with the attributes of God but with the experiences of suffering humans in many circumstances. He quotes with approval "Stanley Hauerwas's suggestion that the early church did not attempt to develop theodicies but rather sought to create communities within which the impact of evil and suffering could be absorbed, resisted and transformed as the people of God waited for Christ's return to earth".[98]

In describing such a church community's theology, Swinton begins with the cross: "God demonstrates power in gestures of redemption that appear foolish and pointless in the eyes of the world."[99] The Church is constituted to practise its own "gestures of redemption", through four Christian practices that offer resistance to evil, one of which is lament (the other three are forgiveness, thoughtfulness and hospitality).[100] Swinton is making a profound and important point here, raising further questions about theories of atonement and ideas of salvation which are also long overdue for descriptions based on lived experience.[101] These too have been the preserve of systematic theologians, philosophers, and the kind of biblical scholars who see no problem whatever in theorizing about arrangements made and deals struck between God and Satan, or God's Son being given as a ransom in some supernatural bargain, as though these things make sense to anyone who lives life at a normal level. Swinson's approach—which sees the lived experiences of love, forgiveness, hospitality and grace (to which we might add generosity, community and the kind of caring that mingles with sacrifice) as being the antidote to death and all that death implies—is recognizable and so, aspirational in Christian communities. These are the attributes exemplified supremely by Jesus on the cross. Swinton is right to correct a view of the cross which wants to claim that Jesus' suffering is "the worst of all human suffering".[102] It is rather, as he says, the place of costly solidarity, which nevertheless undermines and subverts what passes for power and evil in worldly terms. It also helps redefine salvation in terms that include suffering as well as sin. This is how the new Covenant is presented: not like the old one with its emphasis on laws and codes. This is how redemption works: or at least, how it is experienced in the real world. This is how redemption happened for Marie Hargreaves.

Pastoral lament

For Swinton an important first element in the process of lament, exemplified on the cross, is silence. Indeed, according to Mark's narrative, Jesus was on the cross for six hours; passers-by abused and mocked him (Mark 15:29–32), but Jesus only spoke once, and when he did so he cried out (v. 37, the Greek verb *"boao"*, used for solemn announcements), and with "a great voice". This was not just a quiet prayer—it was a great shout of anguish, and a quotation from a psalm of lament, Psalm 22 (Matthew 27:46). Breaking the silence is a key moment in the process, but from the pastoral perspective silence itself is important, respectful and a mark of friendship. Even in other Gospel traditions, stylized as they are, Jesus speaks only rarely in a six-hour period. Swinton is surely correct in adjusting the usual perspective here; this shout he sees as a cry of solidarity with all who lament and who will lament. John's account also makes reference to a psalm of lament: John 19:28—"I am thirsty"—is an apparent reference to Psalm 69:20,21:

> Insults have broken my heart,
> so that I am in despair.
> I looked for pity, but there was none;
> and for comforters, but I found none.
> They gave me poison for food,
> and for my thirst they gave me vinegar to drink.

Could this be further evidence of what Swinton calls "costly solidarity"?[103] In any case it can surely be said that Jesus' references to psalms of lament (as set out by the evangelists) *legitimize* lament in the ongoing life of the Church. This is what theology looks like when we see the discussion removed from the realms of "having to fit in" around the "givens" of sin, Satan and a powerful God.

There are three elements to the relationship between lament and abuse in the modern setting. The first is that lament provides a tradition within which to place the testimony of abuse survivors. This is a tradition that gives permission for rage, gives space for the incoherence or inconsistency that suffering creates when silence breaks out into speech, allowing scandalous questions to be asked and giving opportunity for truth-telling. We might characterize this as *witness*. The second element is the possible *therapeutic* application of the lament genre to help the rehabilitation of suffering people. It is suggested that the writing and performing of lament has a healing efficacy. And thirdly, church *liturgy* can provide a place where the cries of the suffering and abused can be noticed and placed before God. A new focus on the lament of the world in liturgy can both bring dignity to sufferers and counter a church culture which is in denial about the reality and priority of pain, suffering and abuse. Much has been said about witness. Therapy and liturgy are relatively new as practical and applied links between lament and abuse, or mental health more generally.

There is a generally guarded approach to using Scripture as if it were a medication and a quick fix. Nathan White offers a case study from his own experience after being wounded in Afghanistan whilst serving as a chaplain in the US Army; during his recovery, he found Scripture "to be a guide, a comfort and a challenge".[104] What he valued most, though, was not some inspirational moment, but rather the assurance of God's continued presence as he slowly improved day by day. He characterizes this as a growth in "resilience", believing that it "was undergirded by the secure identity already formed in me through years of studying and 'putting myself under' the Scriptures and the God to whom they attest". Sceptical about "crisis Scripture interventions", he favours a more holistic approach: "Scripture cannot be merely a means to an end—even a beneficial end such as health."[105]

Swinton offers a different case study, this time of "Jane" who, whilst not being described as an abuse survivor, exhibits depression of a kind sometimes found in survivors. She is a devout Christian, who also gains support from knowing that God is there for her. Formerly she avoided lament in the Bible, but now finds herself "very much drawn to the lament psalms. It was because I felt like oh, you get it. Like David, I understand what you're saying. It is like the psalmist, he's giving voice to what I'm feeling." Swinton comments, "The psalms of lament provided Jane with a kind of spiritual identification and solidarity with the characters within the Bible, wherein her deep pain was recognized, and her lostness before God was at least shared by others."[106] The book of Lamentations gave her a similar sense of identification. This can be a liberation for members of churches that have tended to concentrate on happy songs and thanksgiving in their services and thinking. It gives permission to be depressed, as opposed to a view that it is somehow shameful, faithless, or not Christian. It has the positive effect of helping to form a view of abundant life that starts from the perspective of those who suffer depression or other effects of abuse.

Megan Warner is a member of the "Trauma and Congregations" project, based at Exeter University. She believes that recognizing the Bible books as informed by trauma provides four important and potentially pastorally useful insights. The first is that the Bible is robust, and informed by the slings and arrows of everyday life as most people experience it. Second, there is an opportunity (as Jane admitted) to identify with traumatized characters in the Bible. Third, the Bible offers what she calls a "language and literature of suffering". Suffering is what brought the books of the Bible to birth, and was how and why Christianity began—it is what the Bible is about. Finally, she believes that the Bible models resilience.[107]

In Warner's view there are two important reasons, as a victim, for reading lament in the Bible. The first is to give permission for authentic speech—to be able to say, "This happened to me". "Lament is a way of combining authentic speech with resistance against the system or circumstances that caused the injury." The second is to be able to frame that resistance within a positive assertion that there is still good in the world. "Recovery from trauma tends to be characterized by an ability to hold together the disastrous experience, and hope for the future."[108]

This will not happen quickly. Warner makes the point that whilst a kind of heroic euphoria can follow immediately after the disaster or the articulation of the disaster, disillusionment can quickly set in and settle. "During this period there may be flashes of joy or hopefulness, but not in a sustainable way."[109] This, I think, sums up exactly the situation of the poets in Lamentations, and the way in which hopefulness appears there. Warner believes that the psalms of lament are helpfully used with victims precisely because they hold together the robust expression of pain without losing sight of a hoped-for future. Swinton gives his own examples to reach a similar conclusion. He recounts how careful and compassionate listening can have a positive outcome, how "listening and lament could begin to enable the practice of lament-as-resistance". As with others, he believes that small, mutually supportive groups are the ideal context for that listening and hearing.[110]

Lament in modern liturgy
Interest in the role of lament in liturgy sometimes results from discussions about therapy—so victims may be encouraged to write their own lament psalms. Swinton gives an example from writer Ann Weems, concluding that "[w]ithin small groups it would be possible to create new lament songs in a similar way to Weems's approach and begin to practice lamenting in ways that are rich and appropriate".[111] He goes on to provide instructions for writing such psalms, based loosely on the kind of analysis we have seen from Westermann: that is, they are addressed to God and contain a complaint and an expression of trust, with an appeal or petition, and an expression of certainty. There should also be a concluding vow of praise.

Catholic theologian Gerald Arbuckle also sees a role for liturgy, but in his case this is related to the Church's shame rather than the victims' rage. He is specifically addressing the Church's role in abuse, and its consequent cover-up. He refers to the need to rediscover "the gift of lamentation" which he interprets in terms of mourning rituals, with reference to Jeremiah 9:17–19:

> Thus says the LORD of hosts:
> Consider, and call for the mourning-women to come;
> send for the skilled women to come;

> let them quickly raise a dirge over us,
> so that our eyes may run down with tears,
> and our eyelids flow with water.
> For a sound of wailing is heard from Zion:
> 'How we are ruined!
> We are utterly shamed.

It is through a process of mourning that new life can come for the Church.[112] Arbuckle sets out an exhaustive action plan which calls for what he calls "collective mourning", which he explains as follows:

> We People of God are overwhelmed with unarticulated grief from two sources: grief from the church's lost opportunities to build a church of collegiality and transparency as specified by Vatican II and grief from discovering the global scandals of sexual abuse of minors and their concealment.[113]

He uses the term "mourning" to denote a set ritual rather than something informal. Such rituals are also an opportunity to remember the "tragedies of the survivors of abuse". In practice this means that:

> Hierarchical persons need to initiate liturgical services acknowledging the evils of sexual abuse and cover-ups that have occurred, and begging God's forgiveness; this needs to be done in ways that allow participants to express their personal and collective grief at what has occurred; this can be done in various ways, for example, dedicating special services in Advent and/ or Lent.[114]

Deryn Guest commends the use of lament psalms as a resource for those who feel excluded from heteronormative churches because of their sexuality. She describes movingly her own sense of loss, as a former Salvationist. The loss is one of fellowship and inclusiveness, the loss of a sense of "home" and belonging, of having a church family; but it is also a loss of familiar ways of communing with God. She takes Psalm 42, a psalm of lament, as an example of how those "on the edge" as a result of any kind of victimization, abuse or discrimination can identify with the longing for God who yet remains silent. She emphasizes the fact of tears (42:3), often overlooked by commentators:

> The tears have an accusatory presence in this psalm; persistently questioning 'where is your God?' But while this is usually posed by oppressing enemies here it is posed by the speaker who struggles within himself rather than with enemies. It is this lingering, painful suspicion and self-doubt that give the psalm its distinctiveness and pathos. The apparent abandonment by the deity is a source of shame and humiliation.[115]

As the psalm continues, former happy days of inclusion are remembered, but these simply emphasize the loss all the more. Guest's translation of 42:7 ("Chaos waters summon Chaos waters at the sound of your waterfalls") bring to mind someone drowning. There is a continuing sense of being abandoned by God and cut off from him. This is the song of one who is clinging to an outcrop of rock above a torrent. She notes with regret that the testimony of LGBT/Q-identified people is just like that, and that the process of rehabilitation and renegotiation is achieved, if at all, "not with the help of one's own church/synagogue, not with the healing properties of transforming liturgy, but in private or in the therapy rooms of secular society".[116]

The theologians to whom we have referred throughout the book are generally agreed that lament needs to rediscover a place in the life—and perhaps the liturgy—of the churches. People reach this conclusion from different directions. Some, like Westermann and Brueggemann (see above, Chapter 6), come from a biblical perspective and puzzle over the loss from New Testament times onwards. Others, such as those concerned with abuse, trauma counselling and the alienation of simply being made to feel different, criticize the churches for an imbalance in their understanding of themselves, their tradition and their role. They are accused of being far too concerned with thanksgiving and praise while apparently in denial about pain and suffering. Actually, that is only partly true. Churches are usually responsive to pain and suffering thousands of miles away in places few have heard of—a pain that is not felt or lived out within the congregation. They are less good at facing up to the pain and suffering in their own locality, and among their own congregations and those whom they serve. If hymns about suffering are sung, they often refer primarily to the suffering of Jesus two thousand years ago without obvious reference to how that suffering is continued among communities today, though there are notable exceptions.[117] Even where there is an attempt at contemporary reference, it is often the guilt-inducing one about how Jesus suffers for us because we are despicable and shameful.

There are two things to be said here. First, liturgy in itself will not solve the problem. The liturgy must be owned; it must be the felt expression of a community of honest sadness. And second, liturgy is more than recitation. It has to be conceived in a way that gives it significance, and that is best done by making sure that it refers to things that matter. I have written before about my experience as principal of a theological college in which groups of students, on a rota basis, had to devise a liturgy on a currently relevant theme. On one occasion they simply chose as the theme, "Things that matter". I was using their experience to illustrate how things needed to be in the contemporary Church, which I described as post-exilic. Reflecting on what proved to be a fruitful exercise, I said we were asserting that worship *has* to be about things that matter. "In these new times worship cannot be peripheral. It cannot be an entertainment. Neither can it be serious stuff in the way it used to be before the exile . . . The exile itself has helped define for us the things that matter. They are the questions of identity, vocation, destiny, suffering, justice, relationship and forgiveness—and our students' choices reflected that."[118] Worship is actually an exercise in practical theology: finding a space in which to reflect on how the world's agenda can meet with Christian tradition in a way that has the potential to transform them both. As the etymology of the word suggests, liturgy has to be worked at.

It is one thing to say that lament is a resource. It is quite another to attempt to locate it within the worship of the churches. Brueggemann believes that the only place left in the Church's liturgical life for lament is in the confession, though he has doubts about the vitality of that.[119] Is he right? Liturgical confession does lack key elements of lament. The most important is particularity. *Particular* circumstances are important when they are brought in human speech to the notice of God through lament. Liturgical confession is *general*, and any particularity is private. But Brueggemann is surely right when he connects lament with prayer in the first instance. That reflects the insistent and persistent articulation of lament prayer as we see it in the Old Testament, even in the absence of any "result". Through prayer of this kind, we do not lose heart.

Lament and prayer
With this in mind, perhaps a better place to locate lament in public liturgy is during the intercessions of the people, where the events of the time and place and the emotions generated by them can be brought in public speech, in all their tragic particularity, to the notice of God with the prayer that he might redeem them. This is where we weep with those who weep (Romans 12:15). As Christ's body, we need also to find a place to lament with those who lament. Within the church's liturgy, the Eucharist is not only the most practical suggestion, but also one that is connected to both the apocalyptic and the Pauline traditions. The writer of Revelation is thought to have a Eucharist in mind in the image of the final celebratory marriage feast, described in Chapter 19 in terms of a victory. Paul describes a Eucharist in detail in 1 Corinthians 11, where verse 26 specifically notes the purpose of the Eucharist, "to proclaim the death of the Lord". It has at its heart the story of the lamenting and crucified God.

It is instructive to consider what that action, repeated every Sunday for millions of people, is in fact proclaiming. The cup of the new covenant proclaims a remission of sins, the eschatological forgiveness that was seen as necessary in the Old Testament response to lament. It is a memorial and, by implication, a sharing in the suffering of Christ. In its context—adjacent to broken bread—it says something about the restoration of those experiencing brokenness in the community of sharing, and also, in a context of the prayer that the drinking of the cup is a way of our "living in Christ" and his "living in us", it is a commitment to continue the work of God. At one level, that means participating in his sufferings in the world and contemplating his sacrifice. Proclaiming the death of the Lord involves hearing his lament afresh. But this is also a ritual of hope for the continuation of the relationships that maintain the world, in the physical sense of honouring those links in creation that are necessary for all life on earth to prosper, and a ritual of recognizing those broken aspects of life which are articulated in lament, and which stand in need of redemption by a God who exercises his power in that way. That is the context for intercessory prayer during the Eucharist. It means joining in a hopeful and persistent community of blessing, which recognizes its ministry of reconciliation as a means of continuing social life on earth. In the words of a modern hymn:

> The bread we offer you is blessed and broken,
> And it becomes for us our spirits' food.
> Over the cup we bring your Word is spoken;
> Make it your gift to us, your healing blood.
> Take all that daily toil plants in our hearts' poor soil,
> Take all we start and spoil, each hopeful dream,
> The chances we have missed, the graces we resist,
> Lord, in thy Eucharist, take and redeem.[120]

That is perhaps how lament might be enshrined in institutional liturgy.

Personal reflection

Lament and redemption: as if
I did not and do not consider myself to have a case for rage or lament. But I did recognize the need to redeem a situation which the outside world believed and urged was utterly tragic. Although I didn't consciously believe myself to be challenging traditional views of atonement and redemption theology at the time, I see from sermons I preached on the subject during Sue's illness that I was rapidly reaching the same conclusion as Swinton. My lived experience was that what some saw as tragedy could be redeemed through love, care, and a bloody-minded refusal to allow it to *become* a tragedy. It was what Swinton would have called "resistance". The world would have been content to see Sue in a nursing home three years before her death, and I was gently encouraged to visit such homes and consider options. But none of those options could maintain Sue's dignity and sheer personhood like the option of

continuing to live at home and to spend time together, no matter how awkward it was at times. Demented people can be very difficult, trying patience to an extent that can, in some documented circumstances, lead to abuse. At least, while she was with me, Sue was safe. I have come to believe that such an experience-based approach to redemption is the way to rescue it from the arid area it now occupies in popular faithful incomprehension.

The question of how to describe hope within the genre of lament is interesting. I am instinctively opposed to an idea of church that involves a lot of like-minded people singing happy songs and hugging each other in a community centre (or anywhere else for that matter). But I recognize the need to take the glimmers of hope and trust in the laments seriously; I like the ideas of persistence and hoping against hope. There is something about vocation and faith that will not let us go—that is a sign of God's persistence. Persisting in hope and trust despite the evidence is perhaps the human response to that. Luke describes prayer as bloody-minded persistence: in Luke 18:1–7, the parable of the persistent widow concludes, "Then will not God give justice to his chosen, to whom he listens patiently while they cry out to him day and night?"

I think I might call it proleptic hope—let me explain. During my time as a TV presenter, I had one series called *Face to Faith*, which consisted of a half-hour, in-depth interview with someone of religious interest (to Wales). I thoroughly enjoyed doing those programmes and can recall most of them (there were around thirty in all, I think). One that sticks in my mind was with Dr Una Kroll, once famous as a campaigner for women's ordination, then as a spiritual writer, and by the time I knew her, a hermit, with a couple of small rooms in a building in Monmouth churchyard. One of the things she said in that interview really stunned me. She said, candidly, that for twenty-two years she had continued with her work with no experience at all of the presence of God. I was amazed, and confirmed with her that during this time she had been a prolific and very popular author; I asked her how those two things connected. She said (according to my recollection), "Although I had no experience of God for that long period, I lived *as if* he were a constant presence [my italics], because I could think of no better way to live." Her life was not lived in cynicism or rejection of God—it was lived in anticipation of

God. The faith element is clear; she had faith with no present evidence. Eventually she was assured of God's presence again, but that "as if" I think is very important in faith generally, if we are as honest as she was. That kind of faith I call "proleptic": it lives in open anticipation, and in the meantime lives as if what is anticipated is true. After all, that's how we experience the Kingdom of God. In every Eucharist we behave and speak as if the Kingdom has come near, and then go out to live our lives in the same "as if". The hope in Lamentations is an "as if" hope, acting as if God can hear and act, because there is no other way that stands between the speaker and meaninglessness. "The Lord is all that I have."

I have also come to take a more benign view of praise in worship. For a congregation of honest sadness, praise and thanksgiving have greater force. The sadness and the joy complement each other and point out the special vocation of each. Congregations of honest sadness must also be congregations of honest joy. I have described my "resistance" as bloody-minded. It would be equally correct to describe it as persistent, and lived hopefully—not in hope of a cure, but simply in the hope that, the situation being what it was, the coming day might be full and worthwhile for Sue and bring her some moments of happiness, the happiness that defeats the evils of fatalism, cynicism and despair; the hope that the day might be a further day of resistance.

The idea of meeting in small groups appeals to me. In Larnaca, we started a monthly series of what we called simply "pastoral afternoons". Each month we decided on the theme for the following month. Subjects ranged from drugs and health issues to marriage and remarriage. There was no plan for the session; people could simply contribute whatever they wanted to in a safe space, and it was open to all. Different subjects attracted different people, and the simple idea was a great success. People spoke candidly and therapeutically. Sometimes there was rage. Often there were tears. Always there was love and support.

Suggestions for reflection

- How do you think you would react to an abuse victim, like Marie, telling her story? What would you think about her return to church and eventually working for a priest? Does that speak to you about any aspect of faith?
- Have you been in a situation that needed to be redeemed? What redeemed it? Did that throw any light on the Gospel accounts of Jesus' crucifixion?
- Is there a psalm of lament that tells your story?
- If you have experienced a eucharistic service, how does the concise description of what the wine might signify, in the hymn quoted above, coincide with your understanding of the ritual or with your experience of it?
- Do you lament the downgrading of lament?
- How important are the prayers of intercession in any communal worship you know? Do they include any elements of lament?

CHAPTER 8

Craig y Nos Hospital

Experience

I was once chaplain to a community hospital that catered mainly for geriatric patients. Many, if not most, had been there long-term, and at my monthly services—as well as on my more frequent visits—they were familiar faces. On one occasion, when I was preparing to take a service, I saw a new face in the line. The man looked like a stroke victim, slumped in his wheelchair with shirt and trousers that did not match: indeed, they looked like hospital-issue trousers. As I came to him, I asked him formulaic questions about where he was from and how he was. He did not speak; apparently, he had lost that facility. I prepared to move on, but slowly he put his hand into a pocket and brought out a small machine, about half the size of a mobile phone nowadays. This was in the late 1970s, way before mobile phones were available. The machine seemed to have a keypad, and I could see that—very painstakingly—he was stabbing at the letters it contained. A small piece of paper tape emerged from the machine as he "wrote", and I waited for this activity to finish. He handed me the paper, and on it he had printed a message. As I read it, he pointed to his trousers. It said, "Before my wife comes, can someone get me a pair that fits me?"

That experience taught me several things. Most of all, it showed up my own failings. Until the man had communicated through his machine, I had simply seen him as one more geriatric stroke victim. What he had done allowed me to see him as a real person with concerns, with a relationship he cared about, and with pride. I was ashamed of myself and have never forgotten the incident. It is all the more shocking to me now, as a result of Sue's experience. I never wanted anyone to see her as just one more demented person. I wanted people who came into contact with her to see her as I saw her: a truly valuable person, with individual character; loved, admired, and with life to live.

Text and commentary

Individual lament is not restricted to the abused. The psalms of lament show us that physical illness may also be cause for complaint. Of course, in the context of the Old Testament, illness was not distinguished from bad weather, failure of crops, or invasion, as examples of God's having decided we should suffer. In a world in which God is responsible for everything, then everything bad can be laid at God's door. But in our contemporary world there are some illnesses, such as cancer, stroke, motor neurone disease or dementia, which are regarded as specially tragic, and society gives its permission for sufferers to lament them. That does create some bond between those people and their Old Testament counterparts whose individual laments specified some physical illness or disability, or indeed the fear of such things: "Do not cast me off in the time of old age; do not forsake me when my strength is spent." (Psalm 71:9). Sometimes the descriptions are quite graphic and detailed:

> Your indignation has left no part of my body unscathed; . . . My wounds fester and stink . . . my loins burn with fever, and there is no wholesome flesh in me. Faint and badly crushed I groan aloud in anguish of heart. My heart throbs, my strength is spent, and the light has faded from my eyes. My friends and companions shun me in my sickness . . .[121]
>
> *Psalm 38 (REB)*

It might be claimed that these are metaphors for spiritual lack of health, but the intensity and detail of the language makes that unlikely. The opposite is true: where metaphors are obvious in these Psalms (e.g. 102:6,9), it is more likely that they are a means of further describing physical illness. In our context, those who lament may not be those who suffer—lament may be undertaken, rather, on their behalf. A literature is growing that explores how pastors and carers can use lament to respond both to the sufferers themselves and to the suffering of those who must watch. It takes us into the area of spirituality as well as theology. There is a community of theologians with a special interest in those with chronic illnesses and disability.

Blind leading blind

The modern doyen of this group is the late Professor John Hull, who was born sighted but became blind in his fifties and wrote a great deal about how theology seems to people who are blind. He makes the basic point that they are easily overlooked. "[I]n this world of approximately three billion people, there are about six hundred million disabled people," he says, "and the gospel is for them also."[122]

In his book *The Tactile Heart*, Hull uses the medium of an open letter to tell Jesus how it feels to be him, John Hull, reading the Gospels. The open letter is, if you like, his individual lament. It has features of biblical laments: the author feels able to accuse God and argue with God; he appeals to an underlying faith, but with a degree of incomprehension. Hull notes that throughout the Gospels, blindness is used as a metaphor for stupidity, ignorance and inconsistency, and that John's Gospel is completely closed to him because its main metaphor is about darkness and light. To be a disciple of Jesus is to live in the light, not the darkness. More generally, he feels that disability is still—in the New Testament—regarded far too closely as evidence of sin, even in John 9 where, as we have noted, that link is disavowed. Jesus says that healing the man born blind should now be an opportunity to show God's healing power. Hull retorts in his open-letter lament, "In other words, the man had been blind from birth not because of some parental sin but in order to create a photo opportunity for you, my Lord."[123] Another interpretation of Jesus' response is possible, as we have seen, but the passion implicit in Hull's rebuke is absolutely typical of lament.

Hull goes on to raise the interesting question of why Jesus did not have a blind disciple. Obviously, there were plenty of candidates around. Jesus generally has compassion on blind people, and his instinctive action towards them is to heal them. Hull has never been party to such a miracle cure himself, so what is Jesus' view of him, unhealed as he is? What he really wants is to be accepted as a blind person who is valuable *even in his blindness*. He doesn't want to be regarded as second-rate by virtue of not being able to see, or to be an example of stupidity and sin. In our own day this is a lesson we are learning slowly. The Paralympics or the Invictus Games are good examples of treating disabled people as *people* first and foremost, with skills, abilities and courage. But in the Bible we find blindness described as a punishment.[124] The one occasion for which Hull congratulates Jesus is his encounter with blind Bartimaeus (Mark 10:51), where instead of simply assuming that this man wants his sight restored, Jesus asks him, "What do you want me to do for you?"—a question that maintains the blind man's dignity. He also approves of the Lord's Prayer because it is a prayer, he says, that blind people can pray. It asks, "Lead us not into temptation." Blind people know what it is to be led; the prayer puts them on the same basis as everyone else. But Jesus never takes the initiative with blind people—they always come to him. Hull thinks that this gives the impression he doesn't notice them. In the end, Jesus himself is blindfolded during the mocking before the crucifixion (Luke 22:64). Now Hull can identify with him, his "blind brother".[125]

This lament is interesting for what it says beyond its modern lament form. Its implicit argument is that lamenting people who have a disability are not necessarily lamenting that disability. They may be lamenting other people's attitude to it and the repercussions for their perceived place in any society, including the Church. As Psalm 38:11 says, "My friends and companions stand aloof from my affliction, and my neighbours stand far off." Disabled people of any kind are not just to be heard, nor just to have their problem solved or healed, but they need to be included, and so to teach those who think of themselves as able. They are, if you like, a sign.

Dementia

Professor John Swinton is currently a leading member of the disability theology community. His book *Dementia: Living in the Memories of God* won the 2016 Michael Ramsey Prize.[126] His interest in dementia derives in part from his prior experience of nursing dementia patients. He agrees with Hull's thesis, but believes that what disabled people in general, and dementia people in particular, have to teach us is something about time. In *Becoming Friends of Time*, he sets out his aim as seeing "what it might look like to understand and experience dementia from within God's time".[127] God's time is to be distinguished from "clock time", the time which has become the master of many of us. Swinton quotes (with approval) Japanese theologian Kosuke Koyama, who suggested that God moves at three miles per hour—the pace at which humans walk. Swinton contrasts this with a doctor who once told him that in his job he has to walk at six miles an hour, and asks the question, "If Jesus walks at three miles an hour and he walks at six, who is following whom?" He believes that love takes time and love moves slowly.[128] He contrasts this with the anxious energy and impatience of traditional lament as in Psalm 13, which begins by asking God how long it will be before he acts, demanding that he act now (Psalm 13:1-3). His further insights on time include, "Time is best conceived as an aspect of God's love for the world"[129] and "Faithful discipleship is slow and attentive to the things that pass us by when we insist on travelling at high speed."[130] Swinton believes that disabled people generally have a better understanding of God's slow time, but he also wants to make clear that this "is not to suggest that there is no tragedy or pain or lament within the experience of disability ... Nevertheless even within the darkest regions of time, hope remains if we learn to pay attention to time in fresh ways."[131]

With dementia sufferers particularly, he claims, slow time is important, but he also shows how issues around memory and personhood are inescapable with this group. He gives examples. On the face of it, leading a service of worship in a home for dementia sufferers is an unpromising prospect; people without cognition are excluded from most of the things that happen in worship. Swinton gives an extended example of trying to get someone to sing a hymn by moving her hand in rhythm to the music. He makes a distinction between cognitive memory and what he calls "body memory", "a meeting of hearts".[132] To lose memory is to lose *auto*biography, but not what he might have called "biography". He compares the derivation of the English and Spanish words for memory: in English the etymology refers to mind, while in Spanish it refers to heart. So, he says, there is memory as passed through the mind, and memory as passed through the heart.[133] The combination of these themes leads to a consideration of what discipleship means for disabled and demented people. Is there a place in the Body of Christ (itself a suggestive phrase for Swinton) for people who are "slow" in whatever way? "Perhaps most importantly, what kind of vocation could they have? How could God call such apparently helpless people to do anything?"[134]

And so the response to our questions about personhood, the response to questions about vocation, and our response to our perceptions of the lament of the disabled, says Swinton, is inclusion. He believes that inclusion is relatively straightforward in a political sense: you can make sure that toilets are wheelchair-friendly and so on, and you can make disabled people feel included in the after-service coffee. But he presents case studies to show that this is not enough. To be included as part of the Body of Christ, people need to be loved. Part of the problem, as he sees it, is that discipleship has come to be regarded in very individualistic rather than corporate terms. Individual approaches to discipleship tempt us to think that we have chosen God; in fact, God chooses and calls us. Baptism provides each of us with "a unique place of discipleship and belonging that is carved out within God's hospitable community".[135] The vocation of the disabled is slow and gentle discipleship, displaying the fruits of the Spirit (Galatians 5:22–25). Hence church at its best, in its slowness and inclusive love, is the true antidote to lament which is urgent, fevered, loud, insistent and ugly. The key words in the theology of disability appear to be *gentleness* (the effect of living in slow time) and *welcome* (the evidence of enlightened discipleship).

Autism and lament

John Gillibrand, a working Anglican parish priest, also presents us with a modern lament in his book *Disabled Church—Disabled Society*.[136] The book is an extended reflection on the experience of caring for a severely autistic child. There are two traumas involved. The first is the shock of realizing the truth they had not wanted to know, and as with the diagnosis of dementia, that can be a long process, raising and killing hope as it proceeds. The second trauma is coping with the child himself, Adam. The book begins by telling his story, and we are invited into their home. If this were a TV programme, it would contain a prior warning about the distress we might experience. Like biblical laments, this description pulls no punches: its strength is its grim reality. It is like the tour we take in Lamentations 2. Initially, "Adam was, and is, very destructive. It is no way naughtiness (*sic*) but he has an urge to dismantle things, to take them apart . . . Adam used to break his [brother's] toys if he got access to them . . . [He] has no sense of personal danger . . . He could not, because of his obsession with wires and tubes, be left unsupervised with any electrical equipment."[137] He had a sleep problem. He had a toilet problem. He was hyperactive and later diagnosed as having ADHD. He had no language. For a time, the family lived in rented accommodation. "In our rented house, we watched him tear down blinds, tear wallpaper, and urinate on the carpet."[138] And so Gillibrand voices his lament: "I am angry in ways which go deeper than aggressive behaviour . . . I am angry with a world in which such things could be; I am thus angry with God, in the way that Job was; I am angry with the Church (and, honestly, with my own denomination) for substituting all manner of concerns for the priority which Jesus gives to the Samaritan's practical care for those in the greatest need; I am angry with the political world . . . "[139]

The book engages with philosophical and religious traditions to try and piece together some coherent perspective from which to view his family's situation objectively. But there are few answers here. This is a cry for witness in the classic lament tradition.

L'Arche

Within individual lament, a theme emerges of hidden suffering. Writers speak to bring something to light, like investigative journalists, only with the additional power of having experienced what they describe, either directly or as carers. The common response is towards inclusion and loving community. A pioneer in this field was the late Jean Vanier (1928–2019). Despite his recent disgrace, it was a great achievement when, in 1964, he founded what was to become an international network of L'Arche communities, by establishing the first at Trosly-Breuil in northern France. He had become concerned by the kind of institutional arrangements made for people with severe physical and mental incapacity, and formed a community—initially the size of a large family or household—in which such people could be integrated with others, to what he believed would be a mutual benefit. This is the most intense example of inclusion imaginable. The underlying Christian philosophy, as he described it to me once, is that we are all disabled in some way. Caring for those with severe physical difficulties can help those whose disabilities are different: perhaps people trying to combat addiction, or to overcome a broken relationship or (ironically) abuse. These are residential communities which assistants join on a temporary basis. I know none who have not been changed by the experience; that makes the abuse findings all the more tragic.

Vanier's classic work *Community and Growth* echoes, and confirms with experience, much of what the biblical record affirms, particularly in the New Testament Epistles.[140] He writes:

> The most precious gift in community is rooted in weakness. It is when we are frail and poor that we need others, that we call them to love and use all their gifts. At the heart of community are always the people who are insignificant, weak and poor. Those who are 'useless', either physically or mentally, those who are ill or dying, enter into the mystery of sacrifice.[141]

A remarkable collection of essays entitled *Encounter with Mystery* (edited by Professor Frances Young, herself the mother of a young man with severe physical and mental disabilities) describes the reactions of a group of theologians to the experience of the L'Arche communities.[142] They demonstrate how reflection on that experience can lead to energetic and insightful theology and encourage new creativity. Taking just two examples, firstly Professor David Ford sets out the key themes he discerns under these headings: the cross, the face of Christ, gentleness, vocation, singing, and the Eucharist. Few systematic theologies would begin thus.[143] Secondly, Donald Allchin provides insight into the Eucharist by picking out the themes of bodiliness, brokenness and humility; he emphasizes touch in the sacraments and includes a liturgy for the washing of feet.[144]

All those who write in this field, notably, write from experience, and sometimes overtly: an experience which they have found both formational and transformational. They point us towards community and to a definition of personhood in terms of relationship. They believe that community should be welcoming, inclusive and gentle, and that it should not be passive or resigned in its outlook, but rather, ambitious with regard to its vocation and possibility. Jean Vanier summarizes it thus:

> To welcome is one of the signs of true human and Christian maturity. It is not only to open one's door and one's home to someone. It is to give space to someone in one's heart, space for that person to be and to grow; space where the person knows that he or she is accepted just as they are, with their wounds and their gifts. That implies the existence of a quiet and peaceful place in the heart where people can find a resting place. If the heart is not peaceful, it cannot welcome.[145]

Allchin quotes, in translation, a verse by the Welsh hymn writer Ann Griffiths (1776–1805):

> I shall walk slowly all my days
> Under the shadow of the blood of the cross
> And as I walk I shall run
> And as I run I shall stand still
> And see the salvation which shall be mine
> When I come to rest in the grave.[146]

The way things are
We are exploring the liminal ground between theology and spirituality here. Theologians who write in this area speak from an experience of being "formed" by their face-to-face experience of working with particular kinds of people. Dr Sheila Cassidy writes in a similarly moving way about caring; her experience is of being imprisoned and tortured in Chile during the revolution that led to the Pinochet regime, and subsequently of founding and running a hospice in south-west England. She says this: "Is it right, I wonder, for me to write about my own experience of darkness? Would it not be better to write dispassionately about the problems of stress and depression in carers in general, outlining the causes and suggesting a few remedies such as counselling, support groups, regular exercise, relaxation and a healthy diet? Oh, that would be safer all right. Then I would be seen as a calm, knowledgeable professional, fully in control of my life and job, and people would say, 'Isn't she marvellous? So strong and capable.'" She goes on to reflect that "The world is not divided into the strong who care and the weak who are cared for. We must each in turn care and be

cared for, not just because it is good for us, but because that is the way things are."[147] Lamentation both tells us how things are and tells us that, in recounting how things are, we find a way to healing.

Cassidy quotes Annie Dillard's reaction to the way Jesus responded to his disciples' question about the man born blind, in John 9. "Do we need blind men stumbling about, and little flame-faced children, to remind us what God can—and will—do? . . . Yes, in fact, we do. We do need reminding, not of what God can do, but of what he cannot do, or will not, which is to catch time in its free fall and stick a nickel's worth of sense into our days." Cassidy comments, "I find this angry questioning marvellous, for it throws piety and pussyfooting to the wind and asks the questions we all long to ask."[148] That is the power of this autobiographical style of theological reflection and spiritual growth, so reminiscent of classical lament.

Rootlessness and hospitality

There is one more group of writers who have been listening to individual lamenters. These are people who have responded to *rootlessness*: one of the effects that Brueggemann posited as resulting from narrative-shattering events, and which is also often characterized by isolation.[149] We have already seen in 1 Peter a response to the *paroikoi* of first-century Asia Minor, but they were—although foreigners—essentially settled in communities and households. There is nowadays a much greater number of displaced people, refugees, asylum seekers and domestic homeless, and some writers have begun to respond to their laments. Here the response is on the imperative to generous hospitality. Megan Warner has offered an insight into codes of hospitality in Genesis, as she reflects on the story of Abraham receiving guests in Genesis 18, and the hospitality that Lot offers to strangers in Genesis 19.[150] Rublev's famous Trinity icon of generous and humble hospitality is based on this passage, and Warner explains that Abraham's responsibility is to offer the best hospitality he can; should that be accepted, the guests' responsibility is to offer a gift on parting. This may be some token or it might be a story, for example. In Abraham's case, it is the promise of a child, a promise that so excites the ninety-year-old Sarah that she bursts into a fit of giggles and asks (literally, in the Hebrew), "Am I to have pleasure?" (Genesis 18:12). The hospitality and the gift establish some kind of reciprocity; hospitality builds relationships.

In Lot's case, he too meets strangers at the gate and offers them hospitality. A crowd gathers as a result. Warner's reading of Genesis 19:5 chooses a literal rather than a sexual interpretation of the verse: the verb *"yadah"* (to "know") can have either sense. For her, what enrages the crowd is not that Lot will not release the guests to the savage sexual lusts of the crowd, but rather that he as a stranger (Hebrew *"ger"*) should be telling them, citizens of the place, how to behave, when he himself is a foreigner. He should have referred to them, the local citizens, before taking someone in who may be a threat to the peace of the city. Notably, he is prepared to put the obligations of hospitality above the safety of his own daughters, on this reading. These two stories reveal aspects of being an alien (*"ger"*), and of the persistent power of hospitality. Hebrews 13:2 perhaps takes the first of these stories as a model for Christian behaviour.

Warner concludes, "[O]ne of the ways in which we encounter God in our lives is through meeting other people, and in particular through responding to the needs of people in vulnerable circumstances."[151] It is important for Christian tradition both to receive aliens, or strangers (*"gerim"*), and to recall the tradition of the Old Testament that Christians are themselves strangers on this earth who, in any case, can never possess the land, which remains God's. We are God's guests.

Warner's essay is contained in a collection entitled *Who is my Neighbour?* We might have thought this a question we need no longer ask, but Bible references are ambiguous. In the parable of the Good Samaritan, Jesus turns the lawyer's question on its head (Luke 10:29,36). In the original command to "love your neighbour" (Leviticus 19:18) it is not entirely clear whether "neighbour" is a generic term for anyone in need, or whether it references a specific sub-section of "neighbours" as opposed to others. Certainly Leviticus 19:33 makes clear that the *"ger"*—the alien, the stranger—is to be loved, and treated as if he or she were not a *ger*.

Surprisingly, these contributions from those whose experience is largely of people who, for various reasons, are on the margins of society's concern tell us something important about what the Church looks like, and how it operates when it takes seriously a vocation to be a community of honest sadness, descendants and inheritors of a tradition of lament. In addition to finding a liturgical place for sadness, it will be a community of realistic forgiveness, of graceful response, of quiet listening, of attentive compassion, of generous hospitality, of suffering comforters, and of loving witnesses.

Personal reflection

St Helena's, Larnaca, was always—and remains—a welcoming church. It brings together scattered exiles and resident aliens from several countries, offering a real sense of community. But having Sue as a member intensified that sense of welcome as the disease progressed. If the church had an anthem, it would have been the hymn by Marty Haugen which begins:

> *Let us build a house where love can dwell*
> *and all can safely live, . . .*

It continues to describe, through five verses, various attributes that form part of such a church being built. Each verse ends with a refrain that suggests what is essential in that church:

> *All are welcome, all are welcome,*
> *all are welcome in this place.*

The final verse gives a sense of the picture that is being presented:

> *Let us build a house where all are named,*
> *their songs and visions heard*
> *and loved and treasured, taught and claimed*
> *as words within the Word.*
> *Built of tears and cries and laughter,*
> *prayers of faith and songs of grace,*
> *let this house proclaim from floor to rafter:*
>
> *All are welcome, all are welcome,*
> *all are welcome in this place.*[152]

It is notable that this hymn is the subject of a special reflection on the website of the Dementia Trust.[153]

When we went to church I had to be there earlier than most, and Sue was generally anxious until the service began. In the early days of the disease, she was still able to speak, but there came a point where she was clearly frustrated when trying to speak, and her vocabulary narrowed until it contained just a couple of phrases: "Come on" and "No". But the remarkable thing was her ability to get caught up in the service as it continued; though she said nothing else, she followed the service and spoke some of the words. She followed and enjoyed the hymns, and "sang" by picking out some of the words and putting a note (any note) to them. Those who sat around her at a service often said it had been an intensely moving experience to hear her participation.

She began a rather strange custom of joining me at the door at the end of the service and shaking hands with everyone. Although that was odd, and something she had never done, people took to it, and it was as if she were greeting people who had come to our house, fulfilling her responsibilities as hostess. She used to smile then and loved stroking the hair of babies, particularly one little Cameroonian boy who was brought to church for the first time the week after he was born, and then every week. When Sue's speech left her completely, only about a year before she died, she would still surprise me: she used to watch TV hymn-singing programmes in English (*Songs of Praise*) and Welsh (*Dechrau Canu, Dechrau Canmol*) and would pronounce some of the subtitles, singing along in her own way in both languages. I used to join her in that, even though these were not programmes we had generally watched. She loved them, and I believe they helped her to have a sense of identity. She somehow felt right in this context: she knew it held the key to the kind of person she was, she knew she belonged. What Swinton calls her "body memory" was intact. She surprised those heroes who sacrificed their own ease in the service to sit with her and guide her. They would often say how well she followed everything; she simply did it her own way, and that way was noticed and increasingly valued for what it was, and what it said.

As to body memory, she was indeed the same person she always was. She still loved ice cream and could eat it faster than anyone I have ever known. She still had a sense of humour: watching the TV slapstick of

Mrs Brown's Boys, she would laugh out loud after she had long since failed to speak. And she did speak with her body. When I came home after a day working away, for example, she would show signs of welcome, even though her sense of empathy had quickly disappeared, and she generally gave the uncharacteristic impression of being quite self-centred. I remember one particular day when Veronika had been with her and had brought her parents, who were visiting. They had been dragged along to spend the day at our house; she assured me that they loved it (and there was no way of checking, since they didn't speak English nor I Czech!). It hadn't been an easy day, but when I came in, a great beam of a smile spread over Sue's face and she opened her arms for an embrace. Both parents had tears rolling down their cheeks. She was teaching us something about communication.

At the end, when she was in the Bryngolau assessment ward of the hospital in Llanelli, the nurses all commented on how she talked with her eyes and how they lit up when she was happy, such as when I came to visit her. You always knew how she felt—there was no need for words. The nurses spoke of her "mischievous look" (normally a warning that she was about to throw her beaker of juice all over them!) or her "determined look". Gentleness and loving welcome had answered her lament. And perhaps I would add another word to that list, a word associated with slowness: patience. Sue taught me how to be slow without being anxious. Veronika is probably the most patient person I have ever seen with another human being. Feeding someone who regurgitates food or tries to knock it out of your hand, or who throws their drink all over you in the middle of an attempt at feeding, is a task that calls for a lot of patience. It is a good thing to learn.

As the L'Arche communities grew and spread internationally (there are now 137 communities in forty countries), a new "spin-off" venture was launched, called *Faith and Light*, which attempted to put the same philosophy into effect but on a non-residential and local basis. Groups were typically based around Roman Catholic churches, but a church of which I was vicar became the first in Wales to form an ecumenical Faith and Light Group, which proved to be a spiritual engine within that church. Their monthly meetings were a delight. Previously "imprisoned" parents of adult children found new life. That such a small thing could have such a great effect was startling. Every meeting began with a service and opened with the same song: "It's you, me, we, that make community", complete with actions and much noise of enjoyment. The group in my parish had dedicated leaders who would themselves say that the Faith and Light experience helped to form them. We did "risky" things: I remember, particularly, a pilgrimage we made to the shrine of Our Lady of Penrhys in the Rhondda, and the monthly discos we ran jointly for our youth group and Faith and Light members.

I have learned that sometimes the pain of grief renders a person inarticulate, needing help to describe how they feel. This is part of what is meant by being a witness. Empathy can repeat what is heard in a different form to show that it has been properly received, or to see whether it has. The pastor can be someone who articulates pain; what they can certainly do is to describe what they see in front of them in an honest way. Lament has poetic form and can easily be converted to liturgy. One role of the minister may, in some circumstances, be to respond with contextual liturgy. In South Wales, there is a widespread custom of beginning the ritual process of a funeral with a service in the house of the deceased. Prayer in that setting can have all the hallmarks of individual lament.

Some descriptions of grief and lament are so awful, describing almost unimaginable situations, that silence is the only response. More than that, silence is the response which pays proper respect to the enormity of it all. Not for nothing do we remember the dead of bloody wars with minutes of silence. A minister can never truly share such experiences fully or be in a position to say, "I know just how you feel". That is not sympathy—that is deception. At a practical level, silence shows a pastor who is prepared to listen, and who does not come to the situation with a list of clichéd answers like one of Job's comforters. Silence is calming; it gives opportunity for gestures of solidarity such as touching an arm, or even weeping with those who weep. Tears are fine (Psalm 56:8). Silence can also be shared. Balancing that silent role of the pastor is the role of giving permission for anger. Often people who want to rage, "to get it off their chests" in that situation, will apologize to the minister first, as if they are sure that s/he will be mortally offended or regard what is said as blasphemy. To be able to say that it's all right to be mad at God is not blasphemy. The lament literature of the Old Testament is full of such rage, which we have discerned is actually an act of faith, but uncomprehending faith. This is where "faith as trust" shows its enduring value as opposed to "faith as proposition", in which God can be dismissed if the faithful proposition about God is contradicted by grieving experience, as if all of this were an objective scientific experiment in which we see how someone will react, if something he believes (because he says it in the creed) is refuted by experience.

Pastors are sometimes so anxious to make sure their funeral services have Christian content that they as good as disregard the tragedy that has befallen the bereaved. They seem to say that it's all OK, really, because of the resurrection. For years I used an order of service for the Burial of the Dead which had as a greeting to the bereaved, "In the presence of death, Christians have sure ground for hope and confidence, and *even for joy*, because the Lord Jesus Christ, who shared our human life and death, was raised again triumphant and lives for evermore" (my italics). That is taking endurance to an unacceptable degree. We want—as pastors—to intervene with sight of green shoots.

For some reason, people seem to imagine that losing someone with dementia is a reduced loss. They seem to think she is better off dead than alive, and that telling me so will give me consolation. They tell me she's gone to a better place, when I know there is no better place for anyone than to be with the one of whose total love you are assured. They look for comparisons with bigger tragedies that seem simply designed to diminish my own grief—what right have I to grieve when young people die in climbing accidents? They tell me that it was her decision—that she decided "she'd had enough". I doubt if that were possible, but if it were, should it make me feel better that she made a conscious decision to leave me? They tell me she is in the arms of God, but I want her still in mine. Almost any words will be wrong, and that is why the silence of God is not a disaster.

Suggestions for reflection

- Can you think of a time when you saw the "label" rather than the human being? What insight came with realization of what you had done?
- Get hold of a copy of the hymn "All Are Welcome (Let us build a house)" and read through its many descriptions of what a church might be. Who is marginalized if any of those criteria are not met?
- Do you have experience of a dementia sufferer or an autistic child? How does your experience compare with those described?
- Who do you think your neighbour is?
- Can you think of a poem that has put a feeling of yours into words? Does that help you to engage more clearly with lament?

POSTSCRIPT

The questions we all long to ask

Honest sadness

I am walking through a small country churchyard. It's a beautiful place, bordered by the hills of the Brecon Beacons. The grave I am visiting is the most recent there and the stone is newly erected. One day it will bear my name also. I take some comfort from the words of Raymond Carver, from his poem "Late Fragment", inscribed upon it:

> And did you get what
> you wanted from this life, even so?
> I did.
> And what did you want?
> To call myself beloved, to feel myself beloved
> on the earth.[154]

I wonder what part lament has played in my journey. There is a juxtaposition between the tranquillity of the place and the turbulence of my own memories. It brings to mind the worst times: the screaming and raging and collapsing sobbing, incoherent, infinitely painful to watch in helpless impotence. And I remember being faced with the realities of life and death and God, and having all the distractions peeled away. And I wonder if Lamentations has encouraged me to share that personal testimony because—perhaps—that is the best way to convey this particular kind of truth.

I am more convinced than ever of the truth of Cicely Saunders's dictum, that the antidote to death is community. But it has to be the right kind of community, and the phrase "honest sadness" describes it well, though true communities of honest sadness also have to be communities of honest joy. If formation and vocation are responses to lament, then I certainly feel I have been formed and that my own vocation has been more sharply defined by my living with a suffering person and learning to respond to her.

As I stand there, I wonder if God is speaking to me. There are lots of books on the market from a spirituality stable, trying to describe how we should listen to God. Some are concerned to dissuade us from simply making demands on God in our prayers, but I suspect that I am not alone in finding it difficult to pin down a time when *God* has spoken to *me* with an unequivocal voice that I could determine as God's. I must confess that I have often felt at a loss, and rather second-class, on retreats where we are being urged to be still and wait for God to speak to us, and from the expressions on the faces of the other participants they appear to be hearing something I can't hear. I have even wondered sometimes if this might be a case of the "emperor's new clothes", and that everyone wants to claim they have heard the voice of God for fear of being excluded. As I now know, in any other context "hearing voices" is a scary thing.

I think I often hear God speaking best through the medium of poetry, or as Sheila Cassidy calls it, "spaced out prose". She writes:

> I believe
> no pain is lost.
> No tear unmarked,
> no cry of anguish
> dies unheard,
> lost in the hail of gunfire
> or blanked out by the padded cell.
> I believe that pain
> and prayer
> are somehow saved,
> processed,
> stored,
> used in the Divine economy.[155]

Sheila Cassidy says that lament articulates the questions we all want to ask. I have not tried to answer questions of my own, but I hope I have interpreted the questions Sue wanted to ask and given her the answers she wanted to hear. What I have wanted to do is to be her witness. And I have found a form and a context in which raw honesty can be uncovered and discovered and used creatively, and indeed, in the Eucharist, even celebrated.

I place my flowers, and turn, and leave.

Bibliography

Arbuckle, Gerald A., *Abuse and Cover-up: Refounding the Catholic Church in Trauma* (Maryknoll, NY: Orbis, 2019).

Balentine, Samuel E., *Leviticus,* Interpretation Commentaries (Louisville, KY: Westminster John Knox Press, 2002).

Blumenthal, David R., *Facing the Abusing God: A Theology of Protest* (Louisville, KY: Westminster John Knox Press, 1993).

Bonhoeffer, Dietrich, *Letters and Papers from Prison (Abridged edition)* (London: SCM Press, [1953] 1981).

Boxall, Ian, *SCM Studyguide The Books of the New Testament* (London: SCM Press, 2007).

British Council of Churches, *Impressions of Intifada* (London: BCC, 1989).

Brueggemann, Walter, *Genesis,* Interpretation Commentaries (Atlanta, GA: John Knox Press, 1982).

Brueggemann, Walter, *The Message of the Psalms: A Theological Commentary* (Minneapolis, MI: Augsburg Press, 1984).

Brueggemann, Walter, *Cadences of Home: Preaching among Exiles* (Louisville, KY: Westminster John Knox Press, 1997).

Brueggemann, Walter, *Reverberations of Faith: A Theological Handbook of Old Testament Themes* (Louisville, KY: Westminster John Knox Press, 2002).

Brueggemann, Walter, *An Introduction to the Old Testament: The Canon and Christian Imagination* (Louisville, KY: Westminster John Knox Press, 2003).

Brueggemann, Walter, "Truth-Telling as Well-Making", in Cook, Christopher C. H. and Hamley, Isabelle (eds), *The Bible and Mental Health: Towards a Biblical Theology of Mental Health* (London: SCM Press, 2020), pp. 105–14.

Carroll, Robert P., *When Prophecy Failed: Reactions and Responses to Failure in the Old Testament Prophetic Traditions* (London: SCM Press, 1979).

Carter, Richard and Wells, Samuel, *Who is my Neighbour? The Global and Personal Challenge* (London: SPCK, 2018).

Carter, Sydney, *The Two-Way Clock* (London: Galliard, 1974).

Cashman, Hilary, *Christianity and Child Sexual Abuse* (London: SPCK, 1993).

Cassidy, Sheila, *Sharing the Darkness: The Spirituality of Caring* (London: Darton, Longman & Todd, 1988).

Clarke, Gillian, *Letter from a Far Country* (Manchester: Carcanet New Press, 1982).

Clements, Ronald E., *Jeremiah*, Interpretation Commentaries (Atlanta, GA: John Knox Press, 1988).

Clines, David J. A., *The Theme of the Pentateuch* (Sheffield: Sheffield Academic Press, [1978] 1997).

Creeber, Glen, *Dennis Potter: Between Two Worlds—A Critical Reassessment* (London: Macmillan, 1998).

Davidson, Robert, *The Courage to Doubt: Exploring an Old Testament Theme* (London: SCM Press, 1983).

Dobbs-Allsopp, F. W., *Lamentations*, Interpretation Commentaries (Louisville, KY: John Knox Press, 2002).

Du Boulay, Shirley, *Cicely Saunders: The Founder of the Modern Hospice Movement* (London: Hodder & Stoughton, 1984).

Duffield, Ian K., "Rediscovering Lament as a Practice of the Church—Especially on Deprived Housing Estates", in *Theology and Ministry* 1 (2012), pp. 8.3–8.5.

Elliott, John H., *A Home for the Homeless: A Sociological Exegesis of 1 Peter, its Situation and Strategy* (London: SCM Press, 1982).

Frost, Stanley Brice, *Old Testament Apocalyptic: Its Origins and Growth* (London: Epworth Press, 1952).

Gillibrand, John, *Disabled Church—Disabled Society: The Implications of Autism for Philosophy, Theology and Politics* (London: Jessica Kingsley Publishers, 2010).

Gowan, Donald E., *Eschatology in the Old Testament* (Edinburgh: T&T Clark, 2000).

Guest, Deryn, "Liturgy and Loss: A Lesbian Perspective on Using Psalms of Lament in Liturgy", in Burns, Stephen, Slee, Nicola and Jagessar, Michael N. (eds), *The Edge of God: New Liturgical Texts and Contexts in Conversation* (Peterborough: Epworth Press, 2008), pp. 202–16.

Hanson, Paul D., *Isaiah 40–66*, Interpretation Commentaries (Louisville, KY: Westminster John Knox Press, 1995).

Hargreaves, Marie, *The Convent* (London: Mirror Books, 2020).

Holdsworth, John, "The Sufferings in 1 Peter and Missionary Apocalyptic", in *Studia Biblica Volume 3: Papers from the Sixth International Congress on Biblical Studies on Paul and Other New Testament Authors* (Sheffield: JSOT Press, 1980), pp. 215–23.

Holdsworth, John, *Dwelling in a Strange Land: Exile in the Bible and in the Church* (Norwich: Canterbury Press, 2003).

Holdsworth, John, *SCM Studyguide: The Old Testament* (London: SCM Press, 2005).

Horrell, David G., *An Introduction to the Study of Paul: Second Edition* (London: T&T Clark, 2006).

Hull, John M., *The Tactile Heart: Blindness and Faith* (London: SCM Press, 2013).

Lathem, Edward Connery (ed.), *The Collected Poems of Robert Frost* (London: Vintage Books, 2013).

Lindars, Barnabas, *New Testament Apologetic: The Doctrinal Significance of the Old Testament Quotations* (London: SCM Press, 1961).

Mays, James Luther, *Psalms,* Interpretation Commentaries (Louisville, KY: John Knox Press, 1994).

Mendenhall, George E., *Ancient Israel's Faith and History: An Introduction to the Bible in Context* (Louisville, KY: Westminster John Knox Press, 2001).

O'Connor, Kathleen M., *Lamentations and the Tears of the World* (Maryknoll, NY: Orbis Books, 2002).

Pattison, Stephen and Lynch, Gordon, "Pastoral and Practical Theology", in Ford, David F. with Muers, Rachel (eds), *The Modern Theologians: An Introduction to Christian Theology since 1918, Third Edition* (Oxford: Blackwell, 2005), pp. 408–26.

Pleins, J. David, *The Psalms: Songs of Tragedy, Hope and Justice* (Maryknoll, NY: Orbis Books, 1993).

Robinson, Theodore H., *Prophecy and the Prophets in Ancient Israel* (London: Duckworth, [1923] 1953).

Russell, David Syme, *The Method and Message of Jewish Apocalyptic* (London: SCM Press, 1964).

Sanders, E. P., *Paul and Palestinian Judaism* (London: SCM Press, [1977] 2017).

Smith-Christopher, Daniel L., *A Biblical Theology of Exile* (Minneapolis, MI: Fortress Press, 2002).

Snaith, Norman H., *The Distinctive Ideas of the Old Testament* (Carlisle: Paternoster Press, [1944] 1997).

Sölle, Dorothee, *Suffering* (Philadelphia: Fortress Press, 1975).

Swinton, John, *Dementia: Living in the Memories of God* (London: SCM Press, 2012).

Swinton, John, *Becoming Friends of Time: Disability, Timefullness, and Gentle Discipleship* (London: SCM Press, 2017).

Swinton, John, *Raging with Compassion: Pastoral Responses to the Problem of Evil* (London: SCM Press, 2018).

Swinton, John, "The Bible in Pastoral Care of Christians Living with Mental Health Challenges", in Cook, Christopher C. H. and Hamley, Isabelle (eds), *The Bible and Mental Health: Towards a Biblical Theology of Mental Health* (London: SCM Press, 2020), pp. 159–72.

Thompson, Michael B., *Transforming Grace: A Study of 2 Corinthians* (Oxford: Bible Reading Fellowship, 1998).

Vanier, Jean, *Community and Growth: Our Pilgrimage Together* (London: Darton, Longman & Todd, 1979).

Van Wolde, Ellen, *Mr and Mrs Job* (London: SCM Press, 1997).

Vidler, Alec, *Secular Despair and Christian Faith* (London: SCM Press, 1941).

Warner, Megan, "Welcoming angels unawares: Abraham, the stranger and the refugee crisis", in Carter, Richard and Wells, Samuel (eds), *Who is my Neighbour? The Global and Personal Challenge* (London: SPCK, 2018), pp. 119–38.

Warner, Megan, "Bible and Trauma", in Cook, Christopher C. H. and Hamley, Isabelle (eds), *The Bible and Mental Health: Towards a Biblical Theology of Mental Health* (London: SCM Press, 2020), pp. 192–205.

Westermann, Claus, *Praise and Lament in the Psalms* (Atlanta, GA: John Knox Press, 1981).

White, Nathan, "Christian Scripture as a Pastoral Resource for Promoting Resilience", in Cook, Christopher C. H., and Hamley Isabelle (eds), *The Bible and Mental Health: Towards a Biblical Theology of Mental Health* (London: SCM Press, 2020), pp. 206–16.

Whybray, Norman, *Job* (Sheffield: Sheffield Academic Press, 1998).

Williams, H. A., *The True Wilderness* (London: Continuum, [1965] 2002).

Young, Frances (ed.), *Encounter with Mystery: Reflections on L'Arche and Living with Disability* (London: Darton, Longman & Todd, 1997).

Notes

1. Walter Brueggemann, *Cadences of Home: Preaching among Exiles* (Louisville, KY: Westminster John Knox Press, 1997), p. 4.
2. Dorothee Sölle, *Suffering* (Philadelphia: Fortress Press, 1975), p. 70.
3. Kathleen M. O'Connor, *Lamentations and the Tears of the World* (Maryknoll, NY: Orbis Books, 2003) p. 110.
4. Brueggemann, *Cadences of Home*, p. 5.
5. O'Connor, *Lamentations*, p. 94.
6. O'Connor, *Lamentations*, p. 96.
7. O'Connor, *Lamentations*, p. 99.
8. Nicholas Wolterstorff, cited in O'Connor, *Lamentations*, p. 101.
9. O'Connor, *Lamentations*, p. 107.
10. O'Connor, *Lamentations*, p. 92.
11. O'Connor, *Lamentations*, p. 128.
12. O'Connor, *Lamentations*, p. 133.
13. O'Connor, *Lamentations*, p. 128.
14. Claus Westermann, *Praise and Lament in the Psalms* (Atlanta, GA: John Knox Press, 1981).
15. Westermann, *Praise and Lament*, p. 230.
16. Westermann, *Praise and Lament*, p. 274.
17. F. W. Dobbs-Allsopp, *Lamentations*, Interpretation Commentaries (Louisville, KY: John Knox Press, 2002).
18. Dobbs-Allsopp, *Lamentations*, p. 25.
19. Quoted in Sölle, *Suffering*, p. 9.
20. *King Lear*, Act 4, Scene 1.
21. Norman Whybray, *Job* (Sheffield: Sheffield Academic Press, 1998), p. 37.
22. Whybray, *Job*, p. 40.
23. Ellen van Wolde, *Mr and Mrs Job* (London: SCM Press, 1997), p. 36.
24. Van Wolde, *Mr and Mrs Job*, p. 107.
25. Brueggemann, *Cadences of Home*, p. 4.

26 Brueggemann, *Cadences of Home*, p. 5.
27 John Holdsworth, *SCM Studyguide The Old Testament* (London: SCM Press, 2005), pp. 99–107.
28 As quoted in Glen Creeber, *Dennis Potter: Between Two Worlds—A Critical Reassessment* (London: Macmillan, 1998). Creeber goes on to suggest that Potter believed "[religion's] role, if it has a role at all, should be in recognizing the *horror* of the human condition rather than trying to offer illusory and false reassurances". Potter also said, on a radio programme in 1976, "[A] religion that doesn't go into the dark side, that isn't concerned with pain, that is something you put on Sunday-best clothes for is of no interest for me whatsoever . . . " (p. 71).
29 Shirley du Boulay, *Cicely Saunders: The Founder of the Modern Hospice Movement* (London: Hodder & Stoughton, 1984), p. 139.
30 The first line of the hymn is "O Love that wilt not let me go"; quoted is the third of four verses.
31 Ronald E. Clements, *Jeremiah*, Interpretation Commentaries (Atlanta, GA: John Knox Press, 1988), p. 175.
32 Westermann, *Praise and Lament*, p. 59.
33 Westermann, *Praise and Lament*, p. 65.
34 James Luther Mays, *Psalms*, Interpretation Commentaries (Louisville, KY: John Knox Press, 1994), p. 105.
35 Walter Brueggemann, *The Message of the Psalms: A Theological Commentary* (Minneapolis, MN: Augsburg Publishing House, 1984).
36 Brueggemann, *Message of the Psalms*, p. 126.
37 Paul D. Hanson, *Isaiah 40–66*, Interpretation Commentaries (Louisville, KY: Westminster John Knox Press, 1995), p. 141.
38 H. A. Williams, *The True Wilderness* (London: Continuum, [1965] 2002), p. 31.
39 Williams, *True Wilderness*, p. 32.
40 See Barnabas Lindars, *New Testament Apologetic: The Doctrinal Significance of the Old Testament Quotations* (London: SCM Press, 1961), pp. 77–88.
41 Hanson, *Isaiah*, p. 4.
42 Robert P. Carroll, *When Prophecy Failed: Reactions and Responses to Failure in the Old Testament Prophetic Traditions* (London: SCM Press, 1979), p. 155.
43 Sydney Carter, *The Two-Way Clock* (London: Galliard, 1974), p. 127.
44 Gillian Clarke (b.1937), *Letter from a Far Country* (Manchester: Carcanet New Press, 1982), p. 19.

45 British Council of Churches, *Impressions of Intifada* (London: BCC, 1989), p. 12.
46 Brueggemann, *Message of the Psalms*, p. 20.
47 Theodore H. Robinson, *Prophecy and the Prophets in Ancient Israel* (London: Duckworth, [1923] 1953), p. 144.
48 Daniel L. Smith-Christopher, *A Biblical Theology of Exile* (Minneapolis, MN: Fortress Press, 2002), pp. 88–94.
49 Smith-Christopher, *Biblical Theology of Exile*, p. 81.
50 Smith-Christopher, *Biblical Theology of Exile*, pp. 95, 96.
51 Walter Brueggemann, *Genesis*, Interpretation Commentaries (Atlanta, GA: John Knox Press, 1982), p. 70.
52 David J. A. Clines, *The Theme of the Pentateuch* (Sheffield: Sheffield Academic Press, 1978/1997).
53 Norman H. Snaith, *The Distinctive Ideas of the Old Testament* (Carlisle: Paternoster Press, [1944] 1997), p. 109.
54 Snaith, *Distinctive Ideas*, p. 102.
55 Samuel E. Balentine, *Leviticus,* Interpretation Commentaries (Louisville, KY: Westminster John Knox Press 2002).
56 Brueggemann, *Cadences of Home*, p. 8.
57 Brueggemann, *Cadences of Home*, p. 9.
58 Robert Frost, *Selected Poems* (Harmondsworth: Penguin, 1955), p. 145.
59 Donald E. Gowan, *Eschatology in the Old Testament* (Edinburgh: T&T Clark, 2000).
60 Gowan, *Eschatology*, p. 63.
61 Lindars, *New Testament Apologetic*, p. 77.
62 Stanley Brice Frost, *Old Testament Apocalyptic: Its Origins and Growth* (London: Epworth Press, 1952).
63 David Syme Russell, *The Method and Message of Jewish Apocalyptic*, (London: SCM Press, 1964), p. 16.
64 Westermann, *Praise and Lament*, p. 271.
65 E. P. Sanders, *Paul and Palestinian Judaism* (London: SCM Press, [1977] 2017).
66 See, for example, Aesop's Fable, "The Lion in Love".
67 David G. Horrell, *An Introduction to the Study of Paul: Second Edition* (London: T&T Clark, 2006), p. 78.

68 Ian Boxall, *SCM Studyguide: The Books of the New Testament* (London: SCM Press, 2007), p. 77.
69 Michael B. Thompson, *Transforming Grace: A Study of 2 Corinthians* (Oxford: Bible Reading Fellowship, 1998), p. 18. Original emphasis.
70 Sölle, *Suffering*, p. 2.
71 John H. Elliott, *A Home for the Homeless: A Sociological Exegesis of 1 Peter, its Situation and Strategy* (London: SCM Press, 1982).
72 Westermann, *Praise and Lament*, p. 275.
73 Westermann, *Praise and Lament*, p. 275.
74 Walter Brueggemann, "Truth-Telling as Well-Making", in Christopher C. H. Cook and Isabelle Hamley (eds), *The Bible and Mental Health: Towards a Biblical Theology of Mental Health* (London: SCM Press, 2020), pp. 105–14.
75 Brueggemann, "Truth-Telling", p. 111.
76 Brueggemann, "Truth-Telling", p. 112, citing Fredrik Lindström, *Suffering and Sin: Interpretations of Illness in the Individual Complaint Psalms* (Stockholm: Almqvist & Wiksell International, 1994).
77 John Holdsworth, "The Sufferings in 1 Peter and Missionary Apocalyptic", in *Studia Biblica Volume 3* (Sheffield: JSOT Press, 1980), pp. 215–23.
78 "The Lodge" in Lathem, Edward Connery (ed.), *The Collected Poems of Robert Frost* (London: Vintage Books, 2013),
79 Marie Hargreaves, *The Convent* (London: Mirror Books, 2020), p. 149.
80 Hargreaves, *The Convent*, pp. 276,277.
81 Hargreaves, *The Convent*, p. 284.
82 Stephen Pattison and Gordon Lynch, "Pastoral and Practical Theology", in David F. Ford with Rachel Muers (eds), *The Modern Theologians: An Introduction to Christian Theology since 1918 (Third Edition)* (Oxford: Blackwell, 2005), p. 413.
83 J. David Pleins, *The Psalms: Songs of Tragedy, Hope and Justice* (Maryknoll, NY: Orbis Books, 1993).
84 Pleins, *The Psalms*, p. 24.
85 Pleins, *The Psalms*, p. 26.
86 Hilary Cashman, *Christianity and Child Sexual Abuse* (London: SPCK, 1993), p. 2.
87 Cashman, *Christianity and Child Sexual Abuse*, p. 54.
88 O'Connor, *Lamentations*, pp. 110,111.
89 O'Connor, *Lamentations*, p. 110.

90 David R. Blumenthal, *Facing the Abusing God: A Theology of Protest* (Louisville, KY: Westminster John Knox Press, 1993), p. 228.
91 So, for example, Ian K. Duffield, "Rediscovering Lament as a Practice of the Church—Especially on Deprived Housing Estates", in *Theology and Ministry 1* (2012), pp. 8.3–8.5.
92 Robert Davidson, *The Courage to Doubt: Exploring an Old Testament Theme* (London: SCM Press, 1983), p. 159, emphasis added.
93 <https://www.eauk.org/changing-church/one-big-idea/developing-a-theology-and-practice-of-lament>.
94 <https://www.ntwrightonline.org/five-things-to-know-about-lament/>.
95 O'Connor, *Lamentations*, pp. 133,135.
96 John Swinton, *Raging with Compassion: Pastoral Responses to the Problem of Evil* (London: SCM Press, 2018), p. 92.
97 Swinton, *Raging with Compassion*, p. 4.
98 Swinton, *Raging with Compassion*, p. 69.
99 Swinton, *Raging with Compassion*, p. 72.
100 Swinton, *Raging with Compassion*, p. 88.
101 As argued in Chapter 5.
102 Swinton, *Raging with Compassion*, p. 100.
103 Swinton, *Raging with Compassion*, p. 71.
104 Nathan White, "Christian Scripture as a Pastoral Resource for Promoting Resilience", in Cook and Hamley (eds), *The Bible and Mental Health*, pp. 206–16, here at p. 212.
105 White, "Christian Scripture", p. 212.
106 Swinton, "The Bible in Pastoral Care of Christians Living with Mental Health Challenges", in Cook and Hamley (eds), *The Bible and Mental Health*, p. 165.
107 Megan Warner, "Bible and Trauma", in Cook and Hamley (eds), *The Bible and Mental Health*, pp. 196–8.
108 Warner, "Bible and Trauma", pp. 199,200.
109 Warner, "Bible and Trauma", p. 200
110 Swinton, *Raging with Compassion*, p. 124.
111 Swinton, *Raging with Compassion*, p. 127.
112 Gerald Arbuckle, *Abuse and Cover-up: Refounding the Catholic Church in Trauma* (Maryknoll, NY: Orbis, 2019), p. 143.
113 Arbuckle, *Abuse and Cover-up*, p. 175.
114 Arbuckle, *Abuse and Cover-up*, p. 178.

115 Deryn Guest, "Liturgy and Loss: A Lesbian Perspective on Using Psalms of Lament in Liturgy", in Stephen Burns, Nicola Slee and Michael N. Jagessar (eds), *The Edge of God: New Liturgical Texts and Contexts in Conversation* (Peterborough: Epworth Press, 2008), pp. 202–216, here at p. 206.

116 Guest, "Liturgy and Loss", p. 213.

117 E.g. "O Crucified Redeemer" by Timothy Rees (1874–1939).

118 John Holdsworth, *Dwelling in a Strange Land: Exile in the Bible and in the Church* (Norwich: Canterbury Press, 2003), pp. 150,151.

119 Brueggemann, "Truth-Telling", p. 112.

120 Kevin Nichols (1929–2006), © 1976 Kevin Mayhew Ltd.

121 See also Psalms 22:14,15; 31:9,10; 62:6; 102:3–5.

122 John M. Hull, *The Tactile Heart: Blindness and Faith* (London: SCM Press, 2013), p. 58.

123 Hull, *Tactile Heart*, p. 23.

124 Hull, *Tactile Heart*, p. 26.

125 Hull, *Tactile Heart*, p. 33.

126 John Swinton, *Dementia: Living in the Memories of God* (London: SCM Press, 2012).

127 John Swinton, *Becoming Friends of Time: Disability, Timefullness, and Gentle Discipleship* (London: SCM Press, 2017), p. 133.

128 Swinton, *Becoming Friends of Time*, p. 68.

129 Swinton, *Becoming Friends of Time*, p. 58.

130 Swinton, *Becoming Friends of Time*, p. 69.

131 Swinton, *Becoming Friends of Time*, p. 88.

132 Swinton, *Becoming Friends of Time*, p. 149.

133 Swinton, *Becoming Friends of Time*, p. 150.

134 Swinton, *Becoming Friends of Time*, p. 88.

135 Swinton, *Becoming Friends of Time*, p. 110.

136 John Gillibrand, *Disabled Church—Disabled Society: The Implications of Autism for Philosophy, Theology and Politics* (London: Jessica Kingsley Publishers, 2010).

137 Gillibrand, *Disabled Church*, pp. 35,36.

138 Gillibrand, *Disabled Church*, p .43.

139 Gillibrand, *Disabled Church*, p. 51.

140 Jean Vanier, *Community and Growth: Our Pilgrimage Together* (London: Darton, Longman & Todd, 1989), p. 179.

[141] Vanier, *Community and Growth*, p. 263.
[142] Frances Young (ed.), *Encounter with Mystery: Reflections on L'Arche and Living with Disability* (London: Darton, Longman & Todd, 1997).
[143] Young, *Encounter with Mystery*, pp. 77–88.
[144] Young, *Encounter with Mystery*, pp. 101–18.
[145] Vanier, *Community and Growth*, p. 265.
[146] Ann Griffiths, "Mi gerdda'n ara' ddyddiau f'oes", as cited in Young (ed.), *Encounter with Mystery*, p. 111.
[147] Sheila Cassidy, *Sharing the Darkness: The Spirituality of Caring* (London: Darton, Longman & Todd, 1988), p. 78.
[148] From Annie Dillard's *Holy the Firm* (1977), cited by Cassidy, *Sharing the Darkness*, p. 153.
[149] Brueggemann, *Cadences of Home*, p. 5.
[150] Megan Warner, "Welcoming angels unawares: Abraham, the stranger and the refugee crisis", in Richard Carter and Samuel Wells (eds), *Who is my Neighbour? The Global and Personal Challenge* (London: SPCK, 2018), pp. 119–38.
[151] Warner, "Welcoming angels", p. 136.
[152] Marty Haugen (b.1950), "All Are Welcome", © 1994, GIA Publications Inc.
[153] <https://dementiatrust.org.uk/wp-content/uploads/2018/03/Let-Us-Build-a-House.pdf>.
[154] From Raymond Carver (1938–88), *A New Path to the Waterfall* (Atlantic Monthly Press, 1989).
[155] Cassidy, *Sharing the Darkness*, p. 163.

EU GPSR Authorized Representative:

LOGOS EUROPE, 9 rue Nicolas Poussin, 17000 La Rochelle, France

contact@logoseurope.eu

www.ingramcontent.com/pod-product-compliance
Lightning Source LLC
Chambersburg PA
CBHW070554160426
43199CB00014B/2493